Date Due

FEB 26 2002			
FEB 2 1 2004			
APR 1 5 2004			
MAY 0 8 2004			
MAY 1 3 2004			

BRODART, CO.   Cat. No. 23-233-003   Printed in U.S.A.

Samuel Adams

The Father of American Independence

Samuel Adams

The Father of American Independence

DENNIS BRINDELL FRADIN

illustrated with prints and photographs

CLARION BOOKS
New York

For my wife, Judy, with love

Clarion Books
a Houghton Mifflin Company imprint
215 Park Avenue South, New York, NY 10003
Text copyright © 1998 by Dennis Brindell Fradin
The text is set in 12.25/16.25 ITC Bookman Light
Book design by Carol Goldenberg
All rights reserved.
For information about permission
to reproduce selections from this book,
write to Permissions, Houghton Mifflin Company,
215 Park Avenue South, New York, NY 10003.
Printed in the USA

Library of Congress Cataloging-in-Publication Data
Fradin, Dennis B.
Samuel Adams : the father of American independence / Dennis Fradin.
p.   cm.
Includes bibliographical references and index.
Summary: Presents the life and accomplishments of the colonist and patriot who was involved in virtually every major event that resulted in the birth of the United States.
ISBN 0-395-82510-5
1. Adams, Samuel, 1722–1803—Juvenile literature. 2. Politicians—United States—Biography—Juvenile literature. 3. United States—Declaration of Independence—Signers—Biography—Juvenile literature. 4. United States—History—Revolution, 1775–1783—Biography—Juvenile literature. [1. Adams, Samuel, 1722–1803. 2. Politicians. 3. United States—History—Revolution, 1775–1783—Biography.] I. Title.
E302.6.A2F73   1998
973.3'13'092—dc21
[B]
97-20027
CIP   AC

CRW 10 9 8 7 6 5 4 3 2

FRONTISPIECE: *In this portrait of Samuel Adams based on the Copley painting (see jacket front), the artist gave him a gentler expression than usual.*

Contents

Who Was Samuel Adams?

*W*HENEVER I SPEAK at a school, a child is sure to ask, "What are you working on?" The students generally seem puzzled by the answer: "A biography of Samuel Adams." Few people have more than a foggy idea as to Samuel Adams's identity, and many confuse him with his cousins John and John Quincy Adams, who were the nation's second and sixth presidents, respectively. Samuel Adams was never even vice president, yet he was one of the most important leaders in U. S. history. In fact, without him, there might not have been a United States.

In the decade leading up to the Revolutionary War, Samuel Adams did more than any other person to promote American independence. He was probably the first prominent American to favor the separation of the thirteen colonies from England. For years he quietly worked toward his goal by writing thousands of letters about British injustice to newspapers and colonial leaders. As the troubles with England grew, Adams was involved in virtually every major event that resulted in the birth of the new nation. He organized and led the Sons of Liberty in his hometown of Boston. This band of rebels became so famous for opposing

British rule that towns throughout the colonies formed Sons of Liberty groups in imitation of Boston's. When a street brawl broke out between Bostonians and British soldiers, Samuel Adams named it the "Boston Massacre" and used the incident to arouse the entire country. After the British passed a tax on tea, he planned the Boston Tea Party and gave the signal for the destruction of the tea to begin.

British officials hated and feared Adams so much that they called him "the most dangerous man in Massachusetts." In April 1775 they sent out an expedition to capture Adams and his friend John Hancock in Lexington, Massachusetts. The result was the Battle of Lexington, which began the Revolutionary War. A few weeks later, Samuel and John Adams convinced patriot leaders to name George Washington commander in chief of the Continental Army.

Samuel Adams did all this at great personal sacrifice. He spent so much time and energy on politics that he failed at nearly every job he ever had. After the war began, the British seized his home. Had the British won the war, Adams would have been one of the first Americans to be executed. But the Americans were victorious, and a grateful new nation called him "the Father of American Independence" and "the Father of the Revolution."

Gradually, as the heroes of revolutionary days died, Samuel Adams passed into relative obscurity. One reason was that his accomplishments came largely through letter writing and organizing political meetings. We tend to build statues of people holding guns rather than pens. There is another reason why most Americans aren't quite sure who Samuel Adams was. People usually seek credit for their achievements. Adams took great pains to remain in the shadows and arrange for others to receive the glory.

For many years before the Revolution, few Americans shared

Adams's dream of American independence. Samuel tried to spread out the credit for his deeds, to make it seem as though hordes of people felt as he did. He wrote newspaper essays under dozens of false names, then wrote letters praising his essays under other false names, creating the illusion that all of Boston was up in arms. He also took promising young patriots under his wing, trained them in his way of thinking, then helped them win high position. Paul Revere, John Hancock, and John Adams all considered Samuel their "political father," as Revere phrased it. All three went on to greater fame than their teacher—Revere as the rider who roused the countryside before the Battle of Lexington, Hancock as the first signer of the Declaration of Independence, and Samuel's cousin as president of the United States.

Samuel Adams always felt that an independent America rather than personal fame would be reward enough for him. One of his favorite sayings was that he and his fellow patriots were acting not only for Americans of their own time but for "millions yet unborn." We who are among those millions should remember the patriot whom his friend Thomas Jefferson called "truly the Man of the Revolution."

D. B. F.
September 1996
Evanston, Illinois

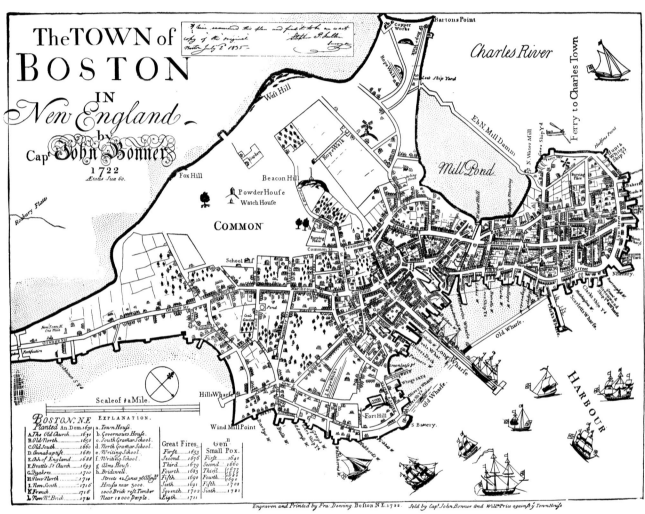

The first detailed map of Boston, made in 1722, the year of Samuel Adams's birth

CHAPTER I

The Young Rebel

MODERN READERS RELISH stories about people who were failures before becoming famous, perhaps because they inspire hope that we, too, may have a glorious future. Few prominent historical figures could match Samuel Adams for early failure. By his fortieth birthday he had seemingly wasted his Harvard education, nearly destroyed the family business, and lost one job after another. He couldn't even feed his family without the help of friends. However, biographers of long ago believed in the maxim, "If you can't say something nice, don't say anything at all." Consequently, we know little more than the bare-bones facts about Samuel's first forty years.

Notes in a family Bible reveal that he was born at "twelve of the Clock at noon" on September 27, 1722, in Boston, Massachusetts. That same day, which was a Sunday, the baby was carried into the New South Church on Summer Street, where the Reverend Samuel Checkley christened him Samuel Adams. All his life, he would be called Samuel, not Sam as many modern authors refer to him. In his own lifetime, Samuel Adams was called Sam only by people who were poking fun at him or who didn't know him very well.

All we know of Samuel's mother, Mary Fifield Adams, is that she was extremely religious and disliked lawyers. His father, Samuel Adams, brewed beer for a living and was called the Deacon because of his position as a church assistant. Samuel was the fourth of twelve children born to Mary and Deacon Samuel Adams. The same Bible that informs us of Samuel's birth reveals that, of his eleven brothers and sisters, only Mary (five years older than he) and Joseph (six years younger) lived to adulthood.

Samuel's family was fairly well-to-do and lived in a large house on Purchase Street next to the Deacon's brewery. One of the home's features was a rooftop observatory reached by outside

When Samuel was a child, the kitchen in his home may have looked something like this.

steps. As soon as he was old enough to climb the stairs, Samuel spent many hours in the observatory watching the ships sail in and out of nearby Boston Harbor.

Boston in Samuel Adams's time was much different from the city of today. To start with, the Massachusetts capital occupied little more than a square mile and was practically an island, connected to the mainland only by a one-hundred-foot-wide strip of land called Boston Neck. Thanks to landfill projects and the annexing of nearby towns, modern Boston is about fifty times the size it was in the 1720s and is no longer nearly surrounded by water. Boston's population in the 1720s was also only one-fiftieth what it is today—12,000 compared to 600,000. Yet the American colonies had so few big cities that Boston ranked as a major metropolis, while today it is only the twentieth largest U.S. city. Shipping was the lifeblood of Boston in the 1720s, and about sixty wharves and thirty shipyards lined the city's waterfront.

In Samuel Adams's time, Boston's streets were narrow and winding, in some cases following paths early settlers had worn taking their cows to pasture or their grain to the mill. Hundreds of shops lined the crowded streets. Although Boston was colonial America's most education-minded town, even there many people couldn't read, which was why shopkeepers placed picture signs in front of their stores in addition to the printed names. Establishments with intriguing picture signs included the Green Dragon Tavern, the Half Moon, the Blue Dog and Rainbow, the Bunch of Grapes, and the Wooden Head. At a shop called the Blue Ball, on Milk Street, the Franklin family made candles and soap. Benjamin Franklin, the fifteenth of the family's seventeen children, worked in this shop and later in his brother's printing house during the early eighteenth century. But Benjamin yearned to be on his own, and at seventeen he ran away to Philadelphia. Samuel Adams was only a year old when Benjamin Franklin ran off, and the two wouldn't meet until many years later.

The Old State House is the middle building in this view of Boston in Samuel Adams's time.

If Samuel Adams could visit modern Boston, he would recognize several landmarks. In his time, the colonial legislature met in the Town House, now called the Old State House. In the spring of 1723, when Samuel was a few months old, the cornerstone for Boston's Old North Church was laid. Fifty-two years later, Paul Revere would order lanterns hung from the steeple of this church before making his legendary ride. Boston Common, the country's first public park, is another landmark that Samuel would know, although in his time it was used for grazing cattle as well as for the enjoyment of people. Near the Common was 150-foot-tall

Beacon Hill, where a barrel of tar would be set ablaze to warn the countryside if Boston was invaded. Today, Beacon Hill is much lower than it once was, because it has been chopped away and used as landfill. That was a disappointment to Boston's children, who in Samuel's time flew kites from the hill in the spring and sledded down it in the winter.

Boston was founded in 1630 by English Puritans, known for their plain dress, devotion to the Bible, and love of education. Religion and education shaped Samuel's early life. By his time the Puritans had become known as Congregationalists, but were still strict in religious matters. Even as a toddler, Samuel spent half of every Sunday listening to a four-hour sermon, praying, and singing hymns. At about the age of three he learned the Lord's Prayer and his ABC's from his parents and his sister Mary. When he was about six, Samuel was sent to a *dame school*, where boys

Artist's portrayal of a New England school of the 1700s

and girls learned reading, writing, and arithmetic in the teacher's home. His textbook was the *New England Primer*, which contained rhymes and other writings with a religious message.

By the 1720s, Boston was not the holy city the Puritans had envisioned, however. A number of Bostonians owned slaves, for it was not until 1780 that Massachusetts would become the first state to abolish slavery. While rich Bostonians spent fortunes on clothing and wines from Europe, hundreds of others were so poor that they lived in ramshackle houses that resembled wooden boxes. Samuel Adams later remembered that as a child he wandered about Boston's taverns and poorer neighborhoods, listening to workingmen discuss the issues of the day. He also made friends with sailors and pestered them until they let him climb aboard their ships in the harbor.

Boys heading to college (which girls could not attend in the eighteenth century) continued their education after completing dame school. When he was seven, Samuel enrolled at the Boston Latin School, founded by the Puritans in 1635 as America's first public school. He thrived on the difficult studies, which included memorizing *Aesop's Fables* in Latin and reading the *Odyssey* in Greek. Why would a boy who would be in about third grade today enjoy studying ancient languages? Scholarly young Bostonians were brought up on the idea that learning was more precious than riches—a thought that Samuel noted in one of his schoolbooks. The values the ancient authors cherished—bravery, patriotism, and perseverance—young Samuel took to heart and later demonstrated to a degree worthy of any Greek or Roman hero.

Samuel graduated from the Boston Latin School in the spring of 1736, when he was thirteen and a half. He showed his parents that he was worthy of a diploma by making a speech in Latin at the ceremony. That fall he made the short trip over the Charles River to attend America's oldest college—Harvard—which the

In *Adam's* Fall
We Sinned all.

Thy Life to Mend
This *Book* Attend.

The *Cat* doth play
And after flay.

A *Dog* will bite
A Thief at night.

An *Eagles* flight
Is out of fight.

The Idle *Fool*
Is whipt at School.

Samuel may have read from this version of the New England Primer, *which was published in 1727 when he was five years old.*

Puritans had founded one hundred years earlier in 1636. Entering college at thirteen did not mean that Samuel was a genius. Colonial people lived to an average age of only about forty, so they went to college, married, and had children earlier than most Americans do today. Although he was no scholar by eighteenth-century standards, John Hancock also entered Harvard at thirteen.

The Harvard routine of the 1730s was extremely rigorous. Samuel awakened at five each morning, in order to be at morning prayers by six sharp. After breakfast, he attended classes from eight to noon in such subjects as Latin, Greek, Hebrew, philosophy, and logic. The midday meal, known as dinner, was followed by a break for such activities as running races and outdoor bowling. The students then had to study in their rooms from two until suppertime. Summer vacation lasted just six weeks and there was no winter break, but students who lived in Boston could go home four days each month.

When they weren't studying, the Harvard students of Samuel Adams's time were a fun-loving, often wild group. They showed what they thought of Harvard's food by occasionally kicking it around like a football. Students were constantly paying fines of five shillings (the cost of three pounds of beef or twenty-five pounds of corn at the time) for such offenses as drunkenness or *mingoing* (urinating) on the college walls. Harvard tutor Henry Flynt was a favorite butt of the students' pranks. By Samuel Adams's college days, several generations of Harvard students had amused themselves by hiding "Father" Flynt's wig and placing snakes in his room. Yet Father Flynt often helped students in trouble, for he claimed that "Wild colts can make good horses," meaning that troublemakers can become responsible adults.

A number of our Founding Fathers were "wild colts" in college; they got in trouble for such pranks as setting off firecrackers in

Harvard College, as it looked in Samuel's day

the dormitories and watching young ladies undress through tele-scopes. There were no such stories about Samuel Adams, whose mother wanted him to become a minister. William V. Wells, who published a biography of Adams in the 1860s, reported that his great-grandfather was in trouble only once at Harvard, for missing morning prayers because he overslept. It was also related that during his senior year Samuel was fined five shillings for drinking liquor in his room. By then, however, he was considering matters that could land him in far worse trouble.

At college, Samuel realized that he preferred politics to a career in the ministry. He came by the interest naturally. At various times, Deacon Adams was a justice of the peace, member of the Massachusetts House of Representatives, and selectman (town official) of Boston. Deacon Adams also belonged to the Caulkers' Club (named for some members who caulked or waterproofed ships), which worked to elect politicians who represented less-wealthy Bostonians. Whenever he was home, Samuel listened to the conversations between his father and the other club members who visited the big house on Purchase Street.

During his Harvard years, Samuel also grew to admire the ideas of John Locke, an English philosopher who wrote about the natural rights of human beings. In a notebook, Samuel copied a quotation from Locke: "It is the right of the people to withdraw their support from that government which fails to fulfill its trust. If this does not persuade government to live up to its obligation, it is the right of the people to overthrow it." However, if Samuel thought about actually rebelling against England as he copied these words, he didn't tell anyone. A student could discuss over-throwing governments in general, but anyone who plotted to do so against the rulers of an English colony might have his head chopped off or be hanged.

Samuel Adams received his undergraduate degree at the age of seventeen and was allowed to continue at Harvard for his master's degree. His parents probably realized that he was as yet unfit for the working world and kept him in college in the hope that he would choose a profession.

Later descriptions enable us to picture Samuel Adams as an eighteen-year-old Harvard student in 1740. He was of medium height for a man of his time—about five feet six inches. His head was large and his eyes were so striking that people who met him often commented on them. They were dark—some claimed dark blue while others said steel gray—and they projected intelligence and kindness. When a person spoke, Adams seemed to listen with his remarkable eyes as well as with his ears. He was an excellent listener. He said a few words in his musical voice—about the Massachusetts government or the problems facing

There are no known portraits of Samuel in his teens or twenties. This is one of the earliest pictures of him we have.

Boston—then listened attentively to his companion's response. If the friend disagreed, Samuel calmly explained the error of his ways, persisting until his argument was accepted.

Adams also had qualities that his friends must have found tedious or embarrassing. He didn't care at all about how he looked. If his parents sent him a new suit, he still wore the old one because it seemed good enough, and he preferred his own hair to the wigs that were becoming fashionable. He disliked small talk, gambling at cards, and most other recreational activities. If his friends wanted to play *town ball* (a forerunner of baseball) or race their horses through the countryside, Adams preferred to continue debating the purpose of government. Not only did Samuel always act as if he were in school, sprinkling his conversation with Latin and Greek quotes, he loved to talk to strangers. While sitting in a Boston tavern, he would join in a song with a group of sailors and longshoremen and then argue politics with them. His friends may have worried that these discussions would end in a brawl, but Samuel became extremely popular with poorer Bostonians. He was the rare Harvard student who wanted to hear their opinions, and they knew that he truly enjoyed being with them.

Young Adams also had qualities that endeared him to his fellow students. If one of them needed a few shillings, the money was theirs if Samuel had it in his pocket. He was generous with his time and encouragement and could be counted on to help his fellow students with their schoolwork.

Samuel was still working toward his master's degree when his family suffered a financial disaster. Because of a cash shortage in Massachusetts, around 1740 Deacon Adams and a few friends founded a private bank that printed its own paper money. Something of value must back money, so the Deacon and his associates offered their land and homes as security for the Land Bank Company, as it was called. The small businessmen and farmers who had trouble obtaining cash liked the bank, but Boston's rich merchants and other bigwigs who controlled the small amount of circulating cash opposed it. Two influential opponents, Massachusetts governor Jonathan Belcher and wealthy Boston lawmaker Thomas Hutchinson, helped convince Parliament (England's lawmaking body) and colonial officials to kill the bank. Around 1742 the Land Bank Company was forced out of business and its printed money plunged in value. Deacon Adams—perhaps the bank's largest shareholder—suddenly owed a large sum of money.

Massachusetts officials wanted to seize the Purchase Street home to settle the Deacon's debt, but Samuel and his father fought off these attempts. The Land Bank failure would haunt Samuel Adams for about twenty years, until well after his father's death, and would leave him feeling bitter toward English lawmakers and colonial officials who took their side.

CHAPTER II

"Poor Adams"

$\mathcal{S}$AMUEL RECEIVED his master's degree in July 1743. It was customary for the Massachusetts governor and his Council (aides) to attend the Harvard graduation. Partly because he had made enemies in opposing the Land Bank Company, Jonathan Belcher had been replaced as governor by William Shirley in 1741. As they sat there looking resplendent in their finest suits, wigs, and silver-buckled shoes, Governor Shirley and his Council may have had trouble staying awake through the usual dull graduation speeches until Harvard president Edward Holyoke announced in Latin, "Is it lawful to resist the government if the welfare of the republic is involved? Responding in the affirmative, Samuel Adams."

Governor Shirley probably listened in amazement as young Adams spoke in Latin about revolting against unjust governments. Although Samuel took care to avoid mentioning the British colonial government, the politicians probably told themselves to watch for trouble from him in the future. Just how much trouble he would cause, none of them could have possibly imagined.

Faneuil Hall as it appeared in Samuel's lifetime . . .

Now that Samuel had his master's degree, he had to find a job. Deacon Adams felt (or at least hoped) that, with his gift for speaking, his older son would make a good lawyer. In colonial times, young men entered the legal profession by studying under an established lawyer and then passing a test. Samuel began his legal studies, but soon informed his lawyer-teacher that he did not wish to continue. His mother, who claimed that most lawyers preferred money over justice, influenced his decision. Samuel also realized that he didn't want to spend his life suing people for debts and settling arguments between neighbors over the ownership of a horse or cow.

As a favor to his friend Deacon Adams, Thomas Cushing Sr. hired Samuel to work in his countinghouse, an establishment that resembled a modern bank. Cushing had high hopes for the

Harvard graduate, who at twenty-one had reached an age when young men began their careers. He told Samuel that he would start out as a clerk but could win promotion through hard work.

Each morning, Samuel walked a few blocks along the water-front to the countinghouse, which was near Faneuil Hall, a meeting place and public market completed in the fall of 1742. Samuel later achieved great fame in Faneuil Hall, but he didn't achieve anything in Mr. Cushing's countinghouse. The clock seemed to

. . . and as it looked in a photograph taken about 150 years later.

stand still as he sat figuring debits and credits in the big ledgers, for the work was too far removed from the subjects he loved—politics and human rights—to interest him.

Cushing's employees were allowed an hour break for noontime dinner. Clerk Adams ate at nearby taverns, where he talked politics with the patrons. During this period of his life, Samuel was becoming involved in the *popular cause*, meaning that he felt the people should have more power, and the English-appointed governor less authority, in the Massachusetts government. Time moved quickly for Adams when he was discussing the popular cause, and as a result he often returned to work late.

Mr. Cushing informed the Deacon that his son was too engrossed in politics to succeed in the countinghouse. After just a few months, Samuel left the establishment—either fired or realizing that he was about to be. Deeply concerned about his son's future, Deacon Adams gave him a thousand pounds, a very large sum of money at the time, and told him to start any business he wanted. Samuel lent half the money to a friend, who had financial setbacks and lost it. Samuel felt so sorry for the friend that he never asked to be repaid. Somehow the remaining five hundred pounds also slipped through Samuel's fingers, with the result that all the money the Deacon had given him had soon vanished.

Bostonians began talking about Deacon Adams's son, and not in complimentary ways. They called Samuel "Poor Adams," because he seemed incapable of earning or holding money. At a time when many of his Harvard classmates were winning fame and fortune, Samuel couldn't even afford a pair of shoes unless his father bought them.

The Deacon then turned to his last resort, hiring Samuel to help him in his brewery adjoining the family home. Whether Samuel actually worked in the brewery or was just placed on the payroll is not known. In all likelihood, the Deacon was afraid to let Samuel become closely involved in the business, for by this time he realized that his son was like King Midas in reverse: He had the unfortunate ability to turn gold into nothing!

Meanwhile, Samuel's interest in politics seemed to be growing each day. The more he spoke with people, the more strongly he felt that the thirteen colonies were being mistreated. The English governors and a small number of rich men who did business with the mother country controlled nearly everything. Except in matters involving their local towns, most colonists were virtually powerless and weren't even allowed to vote.

In late 1747, Samuel and several friends who also supported the popular cause began the Whipping-Post Club, so called because its members tongue-lashed government officials. Besides discussing politics among themselves, the group published their own newspaper, the *Public Advertiser*, which Samuel Adams edited and largely wrote. In the first issue, which appeared in January 1748, Adams declared that the *Advertiser*'s purpose was to "defend the rights and liberties" of those who "wear a worsted cap or leather apron," meaning the working people. The young editor used the word *liberty* often in his essays, as he argued that citizens owed a government loyalty only as long as it protected their rights. The newspaper earned Samuel a few pennies at most, but it sharpened his writing skills and enhanced his reputation as a champion of the people.

In March 1748, Deacon Adams suddenly became ill and died at the age of fifty-eight. Samuel went to the house of the Reverend Samuel Checkley, who had baptized him twenty-five years earlier, to plan his father's funeral. During these visits, Elizabeth Checkley captured Samuel's attention. After the service for his father, Samuel continued to come to the Checkley home to court the minister's daughter. Like other young couples of the time, Samuel and Elizabeth strolled through Boston Common, attended church together, and sat in the Checkley parlor and talked, which was called *sparking*.

While Samuel was courting Elizabeth, tragedy again struck the Adams family. In March 1749—just a year after Deacon Adams's death—Samuel's mother died at the age of fifty-four.

Seven months later, Samuel and Elizabeth were married by her father. Following the ceremony, the new husband wrote in the family Bible: "Samuel Adams and Elizabeth Checkley were married on Tuesday the 17th of October, 1749, at evening, by the Reverend Mr. Samuel Checkley." Then he added Latin words meaning "May it be granted to them to achieve piety, and may they live happily!"

The newlyweds set up house in the Purchase Street home. Samuel and Elizabeth Adams had six children during their eight years together. Three lived for three months or less and one was stillborn (dead at birth). Only a son, Samuel, who was born in 1751, and a daughter, Hannah, born in 1756, lived to adulthood.

Marriage, some claimed, would force Samuel to devote more time to the brewery, which he had inherited from his father. They were mistaken. He neglected the business, which steadily lost customers until it closed in 1769. It would be interesting to know how Elizabeth Checkley managed to feed and clothe the family with so little money or how she felt about her husband talking politics all day, while the beer business gathered debts, but unfortunately her life is virtually a blank to us.

In Massachusetts, the governor decided matters affecting the whole colony, but the residents of each town held meetings to decide local issues and choose selectmen to oversee town business. Samuel Adams regularly attended Boston's town meetings, and at one such gathering in 1753 he was selected for the committee that visited and evaluated Boston's schools. In a town where education was treasured, this was a position of great honor, but it paid no salary. Then in 1756 the town meeting elected Samuel to the paid position of property tax collector. His main task was to demand money from people who owed back taxes.

Had the post gone to the young silversmith Paul Revere, the up-and-coming lawyer James Otis, or the rich young merchant John Hancock, it would have been a much wiser decision. In fact, just about anyone would have been a better choice than Samuel Adams, who was perhaps the least-suited man in Boston for the job. As he visited people who owed taxes, Samuel sympathized with their excuses about why they couldn't pay. He obtained only a small portion of the money, which was extremely risky for himself and his family, since tax collectors of the eighteenth

The wealthy young merchant, John Hancock

century could be forced to pay the remaining debt with their own property. Moreover, Samuel Adams was now failing at two jobs at once—tax collector and beer brewer.

Things went from bad to worse in the Adams household. On July 6, 1757, Elizabeth delivered their sixth and last child—a stillborn son. She steadily weakened, and three weeks after giving birth she died. Her grieving husband wrote in the family Bible:

> Wednesday, July 6th, 1757. This day my dear Wife was delivered of a dead son. . . . God was pleased to support her under great weakness, and continue her life till Lord's day the 25th of the same month, when she expired at eight o'clock A.M. To her husband she was as sincere a Friend as she was a faithful Wife. . . . She ran her Christian race with remarkable steadiness and finished in triumph. She left two small children. God grant they may inherit her graces!

The deeply religious spirit that his mother had helped instill in Samuel enabled him to endure this tragedy. He was as certain that the good went to heaven and the wicked to hell as he was of the sky over his head and the cobblestones under his feet. Later, after he became famous, Adams was called the "Last of the Puritans" because, in an age when people had begun to question religious teachings, he was a throwback to Boston's founders.

The older of the small children, Samuel, was five and a half when his mother died, while Hannah was only a year and a half. With the brewery collapsing, Adams's only possession of value was his Purchase Street home. In August 1758, when his wife had been dead about a year, Samuel Adams read this notice in the *Boston News-Letter*:

To be sold at public Auction at the Exchange Tavern in
Boston, To-morrow at noon. The Dwelling House, Malt-
House, and other buildings, with the Garden and lands
adjoining . . . being part of the estate of the late Samuel
Adams, Esquire, deceased. . . . the said estate being [sold]
for the more speedy finishing of the Land-Bank scheme. . . .

Stephen Greenleaf

This notice meant that in twenty-four hours Adams and his
young son and daughter might be homeless. Among other things,
Samuel had inherited his father's Land Bank debts, which he had
been unable to pay. Now, ten years after Deacon Adams's death,
opponents of the bank had concocted a way to obtain the money
from Samuel. Stephen Greenleaf, sheriff of Suffolk County (in
which Boston was located), would sell Samuel's property to pay
the Deacon's debts.

Samuel Adams was more enraged than worried. He suspected
that Thomas Hutchinson, who had helped squash the Land Bank
and had become the Massachusetts lieutenant governor in May
1758, was directing this plot. Hutchinson was a Boston native and
Harvard graduate, but there the similarities between him and
Adams ended. Samuel Adams, who lived in what he called "hon-
orable poverty," viewed Hutchinson as a haughty aristocrat who
had nothing but contempt for the average citizen. Hutchinson,
who believed that only a few wealthy men should be the colonial
rulers, considered Adams an anti-British troublemaker who must
pay for his father's foolishness. The growing hatred between the
two men would be a major factor in the birth of a nation.

The sale did not occur the next day as planned. Thomas
Hutchinson wrote that Adams "threatened the sheriff," creating
the impression that Samuel stood at his front door with a musket
to defend his home. Actually, we have no evidence that Adams

We don't know who created this outstanding portrait of Thomas Hutchinson, who was to become Samuel Adams's archenemy.

owned or even knew how to use a gun. Most likely, Adams stood there threatening to take legal action against anyone who tried to seize his property. He also picked up his mightiest weapon—his quill pen—and wrote a letter to the *Boston News-Letter* in which he vowed to sue anyone who attempted to hold the auction. The result was that Sheriff Greenleaf twice postponed the sale of the Adams estate, then gave up the plan altogether.

Meanwhile, Samuel Adams was in trouble regarding his collecting—or rather his *not* collecting—taxes. By 1764 he was thousands of pounds behind in producing tax payments. The usual reason for this was thievery by the tax collectors, but only Thomas Hutchinson and a few others claimed that Adams had embezzled the money. Virtually everyone knew that Adams was too softhearted to collect the taxes properly. At a town meeting in early 1764, Adams apologized to the people of Boston for failing at his job and suggested that they replace him with someone more qualified. Perhaps because Adams had let many of them off the tax hook, the townspeople reelected him for another year as tax collector.

The vote of confidence meant a great deal to Samuel Adams, as did something else that brightened his life. For seven and a half years after the death of Elizabeth Checkley Adams, Samuel had raised his children alone. Then on December 6, 1764, he married Elizabeth Wells, daughter of a merchant friend of his father's. The Reverend Checkley, the father of Samuel's first wife, performed the wedding ceremony. Samuel Adams did not want to call his second wife by the same name as the dead Elizabeth, so he used her nickname, Betsy.

Many people wondered what Betsy Adams saw in her husband. By early 1765, Samuel Adams was forty-two years old and had failed at one job after another. He had quit his legal studies, performed poorly as a clerk in Mr. Cushing's countinghouse, lost the thousand pounds his father had given him to enter business, botched his work as a tax collector, and run his family's brewery into the ground. All that Betsy's new husband seemed good at was talking and writing about the rights and liberties of the people—a subject few Americans were thinking about as 1765 began. Yet within a few months Samuel Adams would embark on his life's work: leading his country toward independence.

George III, king of Great Britain from 1760 to 1820. The head doesn't quite fit the body, indicating that the artist used a model for the body because the king only had time to pose for the head.

CHAPTER III

The Fire Is Lit

WHO WAS THE FIRST well-known American to favor independence? Many historians call it a tie between Samuel Adams and the Virginian Patrick Henry, both of whom expressed a desire for separation from England by about 1765. Yet, in his own time, Samuel Adams was considered the first American revolutionary. Clues that this was true include his master's degree speech in 1743 and his *Public Advertiser* articles a few years later about rebelling against an unjust government. Also, Thomas Hutchinson informed Great Britain's King George III that Samuel Adams was "the first who asserted the independence of the Colonies." Another hint that Adams had long favored independence was that he immediately swung into action, as though awaiting the opportunity, when England did something to provoke the colonists.

Money was at the root of the trouble between Britain and America. From 1754 to 1763 the American colonists helped the mother country fight France for control of North America. England won this French and Indian War, but afterward faced a national debt of 158 million pounds, its largest ever up to that time and equal to many billions of dollars today. Since people in England were already highly taxed, Prime Minister George Grenville and other British lawmakers decided that the American colonists should help pay for the war that had made them safe from a French invasion.

The two houses of Parliament passed the Stamp Act, the first major tax on the Americans, in early spring of 1765. Scheduled to take effect November 1, this act directed that Americans buy special tax stamps to be affixed to newspapers, wills, and other papers and documents. Word of the Stamp Act reached Boston by ship in April. The news spread through the colonies like a shock wave. Parliament should *thank* them for helping England to win the French and Indian War, not make them pay for the victory, the colonists claimed. Boston soon became known as the most defiant town in the thirteen colonies.

Several Bostonians emerged as leaders during the Stamp Act crisis. James Otis, a lawyer and politician who spoke so stirringly that people applauded whenever he entered the Boston town meeting, declared that "Taxation without representation is tyranny!" Otis's slogan meant that, since the colonists sent no representatives to Parliament, that body had no right to tax them. In the months before the Stamp Act was to take effect, Americans from Maine to Georgia held meetings and street rallies at which they chanted, "Taxation without representation is tyranny!"

But Samuel Adams became known as the most defiant American. His motives differed from those of James Otis and other colonists, who were truly disturbed over the Stamp Act. Adams was secretly elated. In a letter to a friend, he called it a "blessing," because he finally had an issue over which he could rally the colonists against the mother country.

Adams began writing letters to Massachusetts newspapers and lawmakers attacking the Stamp Act. Betsy Adams later said that

James Otis, who became famous for the slogan: "Taxation without representation is tyranny!"

at about this time she grew accustomed to falling asleep to the sound of her husband's pen. A neighbor who saw the oil lamp burning in Adams's study night after night related that it made him happy to know "that Sam Adams was hard at work writing against the Tories." (The Tories were the supporters of the British.)

Letter writing was just the beginning of Samuel Adams's campaign. He knew that if war with England broke out, few educated men like himself and James Otis would be on the front lines. The dockhands, blacksmiths, sailors, farmers, and fishermen would do most of the fighting. Adams went about Boston organizing these men.

In 1765, a gray-haired, wigless man visited many a shop and tavern. Even if the proprietor hadn't met him, he knew who the visitor was. Samuel Adams spoke so often at town meetings that he was becoming known as the "Man of the Town Meeting." The faded red coat that was his trademark also revealed his identity. Everyone in Boston knew that it was Adams's only coat and that he could not afford a new one.

As Adams greeted the shopkeeper and asked about business, his voice trembled and his hands and head shook, for he had recently developed what doctors today believe was benign familial tremor, a nonfatal condition that can interfere with daily tasks. When he turned to the subject of his visit, his voice, head, and hands trembled even more. British lawmakers, he explained, were plotting to deprive Americans of their liberty—in fact, make them slaves—through an evil tax called the Stamp Act.

Although he might have wanted to return to work, the shopkeeper listened politely to the man who just that past March had finally quit his post as Boston tax collector. The shopkeeper knew that Samuel Adams had risked his reputation by excusing a number of poor people from paying their property taxes and had suffered from his father's involvement in the plan to help workingmen through the Land Bank. Perhaps the shopkeeper answered that, although he opposed the stamp tax, he could not read, so he wouldn't be concerned with the newspapers and legal papers that were to be taxed.

That's where they've fooled you, said Samuel Adams, his eyes lighting up. Speaking as if the shopkeeper were an old friend, he explained that everyone would be affected by the tax. One day you hope to buy land and build a big house, don't you? You'll have to

Artists who portrayed Samuel Adams generally noticed his intelligent, kindly eyes.

buy special tax stamps for the bills of sale. Don't you expect to eventually get married? You'll need a tax stamp for the marriage license. Won't you and your wife want to send your children to school? You'll have to buy stamps for their diplomas. Add all these taxes together and you can see that the British are plotting to tax you to death. Oh, and one more thing, added Adams, seeing that the man was still upset about the British taxing his unborn children's diplomas. Do you enjoy a game of cards now and then? Since playing cards are paper goods, they will require a government stamp, too!

By this time the shopkeeper realized that the British were plotting to steal his hard-earned money right from his pocket. Couldn't anything be done to prevent this? Yes, answered Adams. We are building a patriotic group that will fight for the colonists' rights and make the British officials who try to enforce the act regret it. This may be rough work, so men with muscles and nerve will be needed. Would the shopkeeper and some of his customers join? Of course, the man said, but what will the group be called? The Sons of Liberty, answered Samuel Adams, as he went out to visit the next shop.

The name Sons of Liberty had been unwittingly coined by a member of Parliament who opposed the Stamp Act. In February 1765, Colonel Isaac Barré predicted that "those sons of liberty" across the Atlantic would fight the new tax law. Samuel Adams thought Sons of Liberty had a nice ring to it and adopted it as the name of the organization he recruited to serve as the muscle of the Boston radicals. Since the Sons were involved in some illegal activities, Adams kept his distance whenever they went into action, yet everyone in Boston knew that he was the group's driving force.

Boston's Sons of Liberty eventually numbered about three hundred men. They met outdoors beneath a giant elm at the point where Orange, Newbury, and Essex Streets came together in a rather isolated part of town near Boston Neck. The Sons called this elm the Liberty Tree and the space where they gathered beneath its branches Liberty Hall. Soon dozens of other towns throughout the thirteen colonies formed Sons of Liberty groups,

Cartoonlike drawing of a British official who has been tarred and feathered by Boston's Sons of Liberty

but Boston's remained the most famous, and most violent, of these organizations.

Francis Bernard had become governor of Massachusetts in 1760. Andrew Oliver, a rich Bostonian who was Lieutenant Governor Thomas Hutchinson's brother-in-law and a member of Governor Bernard's Council, accepted the job of tax-stamp distributor in Massachusetts. Samuel Adams and the Sons of Liberty considered this another example of how a few wealthy people tried to control the colony. In August the Sons of Liberty created two dummies—one with Andrew Oliver's face painted on it and the other a horned devil sticking out of a giant boot. On the

Bostonians gathered to stare at the dummies of Andrew Oliver and the boot with the devil's head sticking out.

night of August 13, 1765, someone tied nooses to the Liberty Tree and hanged the dummies from them.

The next morning a crowd gathered at the Liberty Tree to stare at the dummies. The spectators quickly figured out what was intended. The boot referred to Lord Bute, a leading Stamp Act supporter. The message was that Andrew Oliver was in league with Lord Bute, who was a messenger of the devil. The noose around the neck of the Andrew Oliver dummy was a warning of what might happen if he didn't resign as tax-stamp distributor.

British authorities sent Sheriff Greenleaf to take down the dummies. Seeing some Sons of Liberty beneath the Liberty Tree, Sheriff Greenleaf wisely kept his hands off the display. Meanwhile, Samuel Adams, who was among those who came to see the dummies, was having an interesting conversation with Benjamin Hallowell, a British customs official (tax officer) for the port of Boston.

"Who are they, and what does it mean?" asked Hallowell, pointing to the dummies swinging in the breeze.

"I do not know," Adams answered with mock innocence. "I cannot tell. I want to inquire."

Adams had been known for his honesty, but he lied to Hallowell as they stood beneath the Liberty Tree. Even in the unlikely event that he hadn't directed this theatrical protest, he knew its meaning. This may have marked the start of Adams's philosophy during the revolutionary period: If it helped the cause, almost anything was acceptable.

A far more raucous protest, also believed to have been orchestrated by Adams, occurred that night. Around sunset, the Sons of Liberty and hundreds of other Bostonians gathered at Liberty Hall. Someone took out a knife and cut down the dummies from the Liberty Tree. The figures were placed on a funeral bier supplied for the occasion. Several men acting as pallbearers carried the dummies through town as though they were dead bodies. The growing crowd that joined the pallbearers began chanting, "Liberty, property, and *no stamps!*"

The crowd approached the Old State House, where Governor Francis Bernard, Lieutenant Governor Thomas Hutchinson, and Andrew Oliver, and other members of the governor's Council were working on the second floor. These officials watched through the windows in astonishment as the procession walked into the Old State House. For several minutes the crowd shouted, "Liberty, property, and *no stamps!*" Then the protesters proceeded down King Street.

So far the crowd had been guilty of nothing more than a peaceful street demonstration, similar to those taking place in other colonial towns. But then the protesters did something shocking, especially in an age when destroying property was an extremely serious crime. They marched to the wharves along the foot of King Street, where Andrew Oliver had built a hut in which he planned to store and distribute the tax stamps. A few men had brought axes, and in minutes the hut was a pile of boards.

The rebels carried the pieces of the hut and the bier containing the dummies to the Oliver mansion, which stood near Samuel Adams's house. They hurled stones through the windows and split open the front door with their axes. Then they entered the house, drank up the wine in the cellar, and smashed the Olivers' furniture. Those outside built a bonfire onto which they threw the dummies and the fragments of Andrew Oliver's warehouse. "Liberty, property, and *no stamps!*" they chanted.

OPPOSITE: *Boston's Stamp Act Riots became famous throughout Europe. This German etching says on the bottom: "The Americans resist the Stamp Act, and burn the stamp paper that was sent from England to America, at Boston, in August 1764." The year should actually be 1765.*

Die Americaner wiedersetzen sich der
Stempel Acte, und verbrennen das aus
England nach America gesandte Stempel-
Papier zu Boston. im Auguſt 1764.

Fearing that something like this would occur, Andrew Oliver had left the Old State House and rushed home before the mob's arrival. He and his family remained upstairs as their house was wrecked. But when it appeared that drunken men might come upstairs and threaten his family, Oliver stepped outside onto his balcony and asked the crowd what it wanted. "Resign as stamp distributor!" came the reply. Oliver had no choice but to agree. Having achieved what it wanted, the mob cheered and dispersed. Samuel Adams was not present at any of the night's activities, but he may have seen the flames and heard the shouting from his rooftop observatory.

Twelve days later, on August 26, the Sons of Liberty and their friends caused even more damage. After breaking into a judge's home and destroying his records, the mob wrecked the house of Benjamin Hallowell, the British official who had questioned Adams beneath the Liberty Tree. Next the crowd surged toward Thomas Hutchinson's mansion, said to be the only house in Massachusetts finer than John Hancock's. The Hutchinsons fled as the mob stole their money and silverware, threw paintings and manuscripts into the street, then ripped the house apart so methodically that even the roof and walls were destroyed. The lieutenant governor's library was used as fuel for the rebels' bonfire.

The Oliver and Hutchinson house wreckings were the most spectacular events of Boston's Stamp Act Riots. Not only were English officials angered by the destruction, they were frustrated by their inability to do anything about it. The hundreds of rioters couldn't all be jailed, and if the authorities tried to arrest the ring-leaders, the Sons of Liberty might destroy half the town. In the end, the Massachusetts legislature reimbursed Thomas Hutchinson for the damage to his home, but not one rioter was punished.

The Massachusetts legislature was composed of two houses—the Council, which advised the governor on important matters, and the House of Representatives, which tended to promote the people's viewpoint, often unsuccessfully. Oxenbridge Thacher, a Boston representative, died in July 1765. Realizing that he could oppose the Stamp Act more effectively as a representative of the people, Samuel Adams ran for Thacher's seat. He won in a close vote and took his place in the House of Representatives that same day—September 27, 1765. Adams instantly became the leader of the most radical politicians in Massachusetts. Samuel Dexter, a fellow lawmaker, called Adams the "soul" of the House from the moment he entered to the time of the Revolution.

While privately continuing his letter-writing campaign to newspapers under various names, Adams began writing papers for the House protesting the Stamp Act. Now and then he also rose to make a speech in the House. In October 1765, after Governor Bernard informed the House that the Stamp Act must be obeyed, Adams made a three-and-a-half-hour speech in which he hammered away at the new law. Unlike Virginia's Patrick Henry, who stirred the passions with phrases like "Give me liberty or give me death," Adams appealed to reason. Again and again in his long speech he insisted that the Stamp Act was unjust.

"Your Excellency [the governor] tells us that the right of the Parliament to make laws for the American Colonies remains indisputable," Adams said. To this he answered that the colonists had "the right of representation in the same body which exercises the power of taxation." So that England wouldn't actually offer the colonists representation in Parliament, he pointed out that the three-thousand-mile ocean crossing made this "impracticable." While he seemed to be trying to make England back down, inwardly that was the last thing he wanted, so he closed his speech with a vague threat about the hardships the colonists were about to cause the mother country, in the hope that this would inflame the English people.

Samuel Adams was probably the most active lawmaker in the thirteen colonies in 1765. He worked about eighteen hours a day, six days a week, organizing resistance to the Stamp Act in the House, writing letters to newspapers, and directing the Sons of Liberty's activities. He also had a new idea that would aid the cause and add to his responsibilities.

The patriots in each colony generally worked in isolation when the Stamp Act troubles began. Connecticuters didn't know what was taking place in Georgia and New Jersey, and Rhode Islanders were in the dark about activities in the Carolinas and Virginia. In

A number of Join or Die pictures showing the thirteen colonies joining into a rattlesnake were done in revolutionary times. This version by Benjamin Franklin appeared in his newspaper, the Pennsylvania Gazette.

many cases, radical leaders barely knew one another's names. Even within a colony, people in outlying towns often knew as much about what was happening on Mars as they did about events in their own capital. Samuel Adams realized that this was a problem, for people generally feel more confident when part of a group. Colonists in Georgia or Delaware who thought that street demonstrations were too strong a protest might feel differently if they knew that Massachusetts patriots were wrecking British property. Adams began writing letters to patriot leaders throughout the colonies reporting the news from Boston. While he was at it, he sent letters to lawmakers in England who sympathized with the colonists.

Besides all this, Samuel Adams helped James Otis organize the Stamp Act Congress, a convention of colonial leaders who met to plan resistance to the new law. Adams was too involved with affairs in Boston to attend, but nine colonies including Massachusetts sent representatives to the convention, which was held in New York City in October 1765. Although not very fruitful, the Stamp Act Congress helped inspire the creation of the Continental Congress a few years later, much as Samuel Adams's campaign to contact colonial leaders was the seed of the Committees of Correspondence that would prove so helpful.

Finally, the morning arrived that Samuel Adams had eagerly anticipated and that other Americans had dreaded: Friday, November 1, 1765, the day the Stamp Act went into effect. At dawn of that day after Halloween, Bostonians tolled their church bells mournfully, as was done when a prominent person died. Ships in Boston Harbor flew their flags at half-mast, another sign of mourning. Rather than use stamped paper for their legal documents and transactions, Bostonians closed the courts and refused to load or unload ships in the harbor. The story was much the same throughout the colonies.

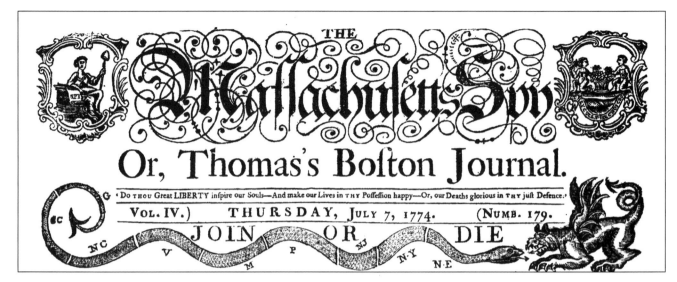

A Join or Die symbol created by Paul Revere appeared on a Boston newspaper masthead in 1774. Revere showed the rattlesnake about to fight a dragon (England). The dragon resembles the one pictured in front of Boston's Green Dragon Tavern, which probably served as the model.

The Americans' opposition to the Stamp Act convinced people in England that the law was a failure. Yet giving in to the colonists was too bitter a pill for many English lawmakers to swallow. There were heated debates in Parliament about whether to enforce or repeal the law. Finally, at 2:30 on the morning of February 22, 1766, Parliament repealed the Stamp Act by a 267 to 167 vote. On May 16, John Hancock's ship *Harrison* reached Boston with the good news.

The repeal created a holiday mood in all thirteen colonies. Even those who had opposed Samuel Adams's tactics were ecstatic. From Maine to Georgia, colonists drank toasts to King George III and rang their church bells merrily. Boston, formerly the site of the most violent protests, became the scene of the greatest jubilation.

Bostonians set aside Monday, May 19, as their day of celebration.

Shortly after midnight, the bells of Boston's churches began to chime, and they continued to peal all that day. Starting at dawn, musicians paraded through town playing violins and flutes and beating drums. Ships in the harbor fired their guns, and the Liberty Tree, where the dummies had hung a few months before, was decorated with colored streamers.

That evening, Boston became a city of light, as nearly every family lit candles and oil lamps and placed them in windows. On Boston Common, the Sons of Liberty launched fireworks high into the sky. John Hancock, the town's richest resident, had his servants place lamps in all fifty-four windows of his Beacon Hill mansion. Hancock held a banquet for his friends inside his home, while for the poorer people he placed casks of wine out on Boston Common. The evening ended with hundreds of men, women, and children parading to the Liberty Tree with lanterns, which the Sons of Liberty hung on its branches.

John Hancock's mansion

Governor Francis Bernard and Lieutenant Governor Thomas Hutchinson were also relieved that the troubles were over. Few Bostonians realized it, but both officials had disliked the Stamp Act, while acknowledging Parliament's right to tax the Americans. Perhaps the only person disappointed by the repeal of the Stamp Act was the man who had fought it most fiercely. A few days earlier, Americans had been inching toward Samuel Adams's secret goal—a complete break with England. Now, people were not only resuming business with England, they were drinking toasts to the king. As Samuel Adams remarked, the colonists seemed to be "mad with loyalty" to the mother country at this time. Yet something few other Americans noticed sustained his hope that the flame of defiance would soon be rekindled.

CHAPTER IV

"The Most Dangerous Man in Massachusetts"

MANY AMERICANS THINK that a love of liberty suddenly inspired our forebears to revolt against England. Actually, the colonists were taxed and punished by England on and off for ten years before they declared their independence, and for much of that time, Samuel Adams stood virtually alone in wanting to create a new country. Of all the Founding Fathers, Adams best measures up to our ideal image of a person yearning for independence. In fact, if we could go back in time and pick someone to organize the struggle, we couldn't make a better choice than Samuel Adams.

The other Founding Fathers spent a relatively small portion of their lives working for independence and had other interests. Benjamin Franklin, for example, was a scientist who proved that lightning is electricity, an inventor who created bifocal glasses, and a writer and printer who popularized such sayings as "Early to bed and early to rise, makes a man healthy, wealthy, and wise." George Washington was a successful farmer and real-estate speculator who became one of the country's greatest landowners.

Thomas Jefferson was a lawyer and statesman as well as a noted architect who designed the University of Virginia, a concert violinist, the inventor of the swivel chair, and the originator of our monetary system in which we use dollars and cents. Paul Revere was a gifted artist and silversmith whose church bells and tableware are of great value today. Other men who helped found the nation were prominent lawyers, doctors, and businessmen.

Samuel Adams, on the other hand, had no successful career outside politics, no close friends other than his political associates, and no hobbies. He seems to have never hunted or fished, two popular activities in colonial times, and in an age when the horse was the leading means of transportation, it was said that he didn't know how to ride. William V. Wells, in his biography *The Life and Public Services of Samuel Adams*, spends just a page describing his great-grandfather's leisure activities, which consisted of singing with his family, sailing with John Hancock now and then, and exploring a cave near Boston with John Adams on one occasion. Wells devotes the other 1,452 pages to Samuel Adams's unceasing work for "American Independence, the one aim of his life."

Adams's desire for independence was driven by his dream of America's potential. England by the mid-eighteenth century, in his view, was decaying. The mother country had widespread poverty, an educational system that neglected the poor, and a legal system in which people without influence and money could not obtain a fair trial. The America Samuel Adams envisioned would be a much better place. There every child would be educated, justice would be dealt fairly to all, and lawmakers would view officeholding as a public service. This would come about, he felt, because Americans wanted to be a virtuous people. On several occasions before the Revolution, Samuel Adams described his vision for the country. Writing to a friend, he declared, "Providence [God] will erect a mighty empire in America," and in a letter to the *Boston Gazette*, he gazed into the future and predicted:

> No people that ever trod the stage of the world have had so glorious a prospect as now rises before the Americans. There is nothing good or great but their wisdom may acquire, and to what heights they will arrive in the progress of time no one can conceive.

The little-noticed event that lifted Samuel Adams's spirits was a law passed by Parliament at the same time that it repealed the Stamp Act in 1766. Called the Declaratory Act, it asserted Parliament's right to make laws for the thirteen colonies "in all cases whatsoever." Most Americans who were aware of the Declaratory Act assumed the British just wanted to show they were still in charge and wouldn't tax them further. Samuel Adams hoped it meant that more oppressive taxes would be forthcoming.

While awaiting England's next move, Adams reminded Americans of other British injustices. "Where there is a spark of patriotic fire, we will enkindle it!" was his motto. For example, he pointed out that many colonial officials held several posts at once. Thomas Hutchinson was lieutenant governor, as well as a member of Governor Francis Bernard's Council and a judge. In 1766, Adams led a successful fight to have Hutchinson removed from the governor's Council. His hatred for Adams deepening, Hutchinson began referring to him as "the Grand Incendiary," meaning someone who sets fires or stirs up trouble.

Samuel Adams was also forming new political friendships at this time. One was with John Hancock, a merchant fourteen years his junior. When John was seven his father died, and his mother sent him to Boston to live with his wealthy uncle and aunt. Thomas and Lydia Hancock sent John to Harvard, bought him everything he wanted, and doted on him. When Uncle Thomas died in 1764 he left his twenty-seven-year-old nephew a fortune, making him one of New England's richest men. But losing his father and leaving his mother as a child scarred John Hancock in a way that time never healed. All his life, he couldn't satisfy his craving for love and praise.

Hancock reveled in his wealth. He bought enough suits, shoes, and hats to open a clothing store, drove about Boston in a magnificent carriage, and gave parties that were the talk of the Massachusetts capital. Yet John was as known for his generosity as he was for his showy way of life. Each winter he donated food and firewood to Boston's poor. After a fire struck Boston in 1767, he helped rebuild the damaged structures. When the black American Phillis Wheatley wrote a book of poetry just before the Revolutionary War, Hancock helped arrange for its publication. Although no great thinker himself, Hancock respected brilliant people and followed their lead if convinced of the justness of their cause. Hancock was brave, too—the kind of man who would leap off a bridge without hesitation to save a drowning person.

Adams knew all this, and he also knew Hancock's drawbacks. Because of his need to be idolized, the young merchant loved it when crowds ran alongside his coach yelling "King Hancock!" He was easily insulted and became childish at times. Hancock could also shift loyalties if someone came along who gave him more praise.

Samuel Adams realized that Hancock would be a valuable addition to the Liberty Party, as the radicals now called themselves. Many people viewed the party as the refuge of the penniless, the lawless, and the insane. Samuel Adams, its main leader, helped account for the penniless part of the image. The Sons of Liberty provided the lawless reputation. James Otis, who at times had to be taken out to the country because of mental illness, inspired the gossip about the party being a haven for disturbed people. If rich, law-abiding, and rather well-adjusted John Hancock joined the Liberty Party, he might lure more people like himself to join it.

Adams began taking Hancock with him to his political clubs and meetings. They were an odd-looking pair—the older man in his one threadbare suit and the elegant young merchant who was Boston's most eligible bachelor. Hancock felt proud to associate with a man he considered America's greatest political genius. While outwardly returning Hancock's affection, Samuel Adams could not truly respect a man who was so in love with riches. It may seem ruthless that Adams used Hancock to advance the cause, yet we "millions yet unborn," as Samuel called us, might not enjoy American independence had he not done what was necessary to achieve it.

Before the election of 1766, the Liberty Party was poring over a list of men who wanted to represent Boston in the Massachusetts House. When they reached the name of merchant John Rowe, Samuel Adams glanced toward Hancock's Beacon Hill mansion and asked, "Is there not another John that may do better?" John Hancock became a candidate and won the election. Within hours, Samuel and John Adams were crossing Boston Common when Hancock's mansion came into view. "This town has done a wise thing today," Samuel told his cousin. When John asked what he meant, Samuel answered, "They have made that young man's fortune their own."

John Adams was much more Samuel's kind of man than John Hancock. Although the two Adamses were second cousins and both were Harvard graduates, they had spent little time together until about 1765. John was thirteen years younger than Samuel and had lived in his hometown of Braintree, a few miles from Boston, until his thirties. However, John was a lawyer, and as

Samuel's cousin John Adams

legal business took him into Boston, the cousins grew closer. They even began calling each other "my brother Samuel" and "my brother John," fooling many people into thinking they really were brothers. As yet, John was much less rebellious than his cousin, for the lawyer in him weighed things carefully before making major decisions, but Samuel felt that John had tremendous potential to help the cause. In his debating ability and knowledge of the law, John Adams had no equal in Massachusetts. A gigantic ego was his cousin John's greatest weakness, in Samuel's view. So certain was John Adams of his future greatness that he could hardly sneeze without making a note about it.

By about 1766, Samuel Adams was grooming a number of other bright young men for the Liberty Party. Thanks to a description provided by his cousin, we know how Samuel operated. "Samuel Adams," wrote John Adams, "made it his constant rule to watch the rise of every brilliant genius, to seek his acquaintance, to court his friendship, to cultivate his natural feelings in favor of his native country, to warn him against the hostile designs of Great Britain, and to fix his affections and reflections on the side of his native country. I could enumerate a list, but I will confine myself to a few." John Hancock headed his list. Also on it were Samuel Adams's family physician, Dr. Joseph Warren, who neglected medicine in favor of politics, and Josiah Quincy, a legal colleague of John Adams. These and many other young men considered Samuel Adams their "political father," as Paul Revere once said.

Adams and his political sons were ready when the mother country made its next move. In the spring of 1767, British treasurer

Dr. Joseph Warren

Charles Townshend convinced Parliament to pass the Townshend Acts, which taxed paint, tea, lead, paper, and glass brought into the colonies. Around then, Britain also decided to enforce the Navigation Acts, which made it difficult for Americans to trade legally with any nation but England. Previously, the mother country had not much cared when the colonists defied the Navigation Acts by smuggling goods from non-British nations into American ports.

Although Samuel Adams acted as though he were the most outraged person in America, the Townshend Acts were the answer to his prayers. Once again he wrote letters to newspapers, scheduled protest meetings, and directed the Sons of Liberty to hang dummies of British officials from the Liberty Tree. He also organized a campaign to keep British-made goods out of Massachusetts. This would cost British merchants a fortune, Adams hoped, and turn them against their own government. By the fall of 1767, the Boston town meeting and the Massachusetts legislature had both adopted Adams's strategy to boycott British goods, and other colonies followed suit.

Boston's Sons of Liberty prowled the streets looking for merchants who broke the boycott. Gangs of boys—the sons of the Sons of Liberty—went about smashing these merchants' windows and smearing their walls with *night soil*, a polite term for excrement. Signs with the word IMPORTER were also placed in front of establishments that continued to trade with England. If all this failed to impress the offender, he might be kidnapped on his way home from work and coated with hot tar and feathers, a form of torture that often left scars on the victim's body.

In early 1768, the Massachusetts House of Representatives asked Adams to write several letters to officials in England complaining about the Townshend taxes. One January night when he was writing the most important of these papers, the Petition to the King, his twelve-year-old daughter, Hannah, entered his study and asked if the document might actually be touched by His Majesty's hands. "It will more likely be spurned by the royal foot, my dear," her father answered, according to Hannah's later recollections. Samuel Adams knew that King George III was so enraged at the colonists that he generally ignored their petitions.

A few months later, Boston was the site of a clash reminiscent of the Stamp Act Riots. Uncle Thomas Hancock had made part of the family fortune the old-fashioned American way: by smuggling. His ship captains had purchased goods from non-British countries and then smuggled them into Boston without the British authorities taking much notice. Bostonians were generally pleased about this, for the smuggled goods sold for less than similar items shipped legally from England. Although merchants in the mother country were disturbed about losing their stranglehold on the American market, they were three thousand miles away and could do little about it.

John Hancock continued his family's smuggling tradition. On May 9, 1768, his new ship, the *Liberty*, arrived at Hancock's Wharf carrying more than a hundred casks of expensive wine smuggled from Portugal's Madeira Islands. Recently Hancock had vowed in the Massachusetts House that any customs official who tried to inspect his ships would regret it. He kept his word. Suspecting that the *Liberty* contained smuggled goods, a customs officer boarded the vessel soon after its arrival. Hancock's men threw him into a cabin and nailed it shut. The officer was not set free until Hancock's crew had unloaded the smuggled goods.

British officials decided to make an example of Hancock, especially since their warship *Romney* was in Boston Harbor to help enforce the Navigation Acts. On June 10, 1768, two British customs officers, Joseph Harrison and Benjamin Hallowell (whose home had been wrecked by the Sons of Liberty three years earlier), boarded Hancock's ship and placed the King's Broad Arrow on it. This sign meant that the *Liberty* and its cargo belonged to King George III as punishment for Hancock's smuggling. At Hallowell's signal, boatloads of British marines from the *Romney* rowed out to the *Liberty* and towed it back to their warship. They cabled the *Liberty* to the *Romney* so that the Sons of Liberty could not retrieve the vessel for Hancock.

Meanwhile, a crowd of about five hundred angry dockworkers and other admirers of John Hancock gathered at Hancock's Wharf. When Hallowell and Harrison tried to return to their homes, the mob threw bricks at them, smashed their windows, and stole a boat belonging to Harrison. They dragged the boat to Boston Common and burned it as a kind of offering to John Hancock a short way from his mansion.

The Loyalists (as pro-British Americans were starting to call themselves) and British officials were certain that Samuel Adams was behind this and every other rebellious act in Boston in 1768. That year Governor Francis Bernard called Adams "the most dangerous man in Massachusetts, a man dedicated to the perpetration of mischief." Peter Oliver, a Loyalist who like his brother Andrew Oliver was related to Thomas Hutchinson by marriage, was even more insulting. If one "wished to draw the Picture of the Devil," wrote Oliver, "Sam Adams [should] sit for him." As for Thomas Hutchinson, his hatred for the man he called "the Grand Incendiary" was becoming an obsession. Fearful that Adams had the power to direct Americans to begin a revolution, Hutchinson coined yet another nickname for him: "The Master of the Puppets."

The Loyalists were so certain that Hancock was under Adams's control that they called him "Johnny Dupe" and joked that Samuel "led him around like an ape." They also claimed that Hancock had "deep pockets and shallow brains," implying that he gave money to the patriot cause at Adams's bidding. But to the patriots, Hancock was a hero for fighting the British at the cost of the *Liberty*, which was never returned to him. For more than two centuries, the extent of Samuel Adams's involvement in the *Liberty* affair has remained a mystery.

Because of all the tumult in Boston, officials in England decided to send in soldiers to restore order. Upon learning of this in the summer of 1768, most Bostonians dreaded the prospect, for the mixture of troops and patriots could ignite a far more violent explosion than the Stamp Act and *Liberty* riots. Samuel Adams was delighted, for although he didn't want people to die, what better way to rally Americans to the cause than for the British to attack innocent Bostonians?

The British troops reached Boston Harbor in the early fall. For several weeks they remained aboard their ships while preparations were completed onshore. Governor Bernard ordered the

Woodcut by Paul Revere showing the landing of the British troops in the fall of 1768

legislature to adjourn and had the beacon taken down from Beacon Hill to prevent Bostonians from alerting the countryside to the soldiers' arrival.

Meanwhile, Samuel Adams was planning a colonywide convention to discuss the situation. In mid-September 1768 he sent horseback riders to deliver invitations to every one of the colony's more than three hundred towns. About a hundred towns sent representatives to the meeting, which opened on September 22 in Faneuil Hall. Shortly after the convention began, Governor Bernard ordered the delegates to return home. Much to Samuel Adams's pleasure, they defied the order. However, partly because the inland towns weren't much concerned about the English troops in Boston Harbor, the convention produced only the usual petitions to British officials.

On October 1 the soldiers from Europe's strongest nation came ashore in a manner intended to awe the Bostonians. While cannons on the transport ships thundered a salute, the seven hundred soldiers in red coats and cocked hats marched into town with their muskets on their shoulders. Paul Revere, who left his silversmith shop to join the onlookers, wrote about the spectacle: "[They] marched with insolent parade, drums beating, fifes playing, up King Street, each soldier having received sixteen rounds of powder and ball." Revere's last comment meant that each soldier carried enough ammunition to fire sixteen musket shots. The arrival of more transport vessels soon raised the number of redcoats to four thousand, or about one soldier for every adult man in town.

British leaders hoped that Boston's Loyalists would house the soldiers, but they were reluctant to do so because they knew the Sons of Liberty would seek revenge once the redcoats departed. Some of the soldiers had to pitch tents on Boston Common, while others were quartered in Faneuil Hall and in old warehouses. The redcoats set up cannons and aimed them at the Old State House, where the Massachusetts legislature met, and at other strategic spots. The soldiers also annoyed the townspeople by stopping them on the street to ask where they were going and by marching at odd hours. John Adams, who had moved into Boston with his family earlier that year, wrote that a regiment of redcoats drilled regularly near his front door.

Samuel Adams decided that the wisest strategy was to harass the redcoats while making them appear to the world as bullies. "Put your enemy in the wrong, and keep him so," he explained in a letter to John Augustine Washington, a younger brother of George Washington. Adams's letters to the Boston newspapers were his angriest, most emotional writing to date. In one letter published in the *Boston Gazette* in 1769 he called the redcoats "locusts and caterpillars" and then said:

> An army of soldiers must be stationed in our very bowels! . . . In this dilemma, to what a dreadful alternative are we reduced—*to resist this tyranny, or submit to chains*! . . . God forbid that free countries should ever again yield to tyranny! This has long been the unhappy fate of the world, while it was overspread with ignorance and enveloped in darkness. Mankind, I hope, are now become too enlightened to suffer it much longer.

Like all good newspapers, the Boston papers of the 1760s tried to print the truth. This didn't suit Adams's purpose, so in September 1768 he began the *Journal of Events*, which contained accounts of how the redcoats were beating up the men of Boston and raping their wives and daughters. Many Bostonians realized that Samuel Adams had concocted quite a few of these stories, but the paper wasn't meant for the Massachusetts capital

alone. Adams sent copies of the *Journal* to newspapers through-out the thirteen colonies, which reprinted his articles. People in other colonies read the accounts and were incensed at the British without suspecting that the stories weren't true.

Adams and his followers also used children to taunt the red-coats in ways that would have been dangerous for adults to do. The children went about Boston yelling "Lobsterbacks!" and "Bloodybacks!" at the redcoats, while occasionally throwing rotten eggs or rocks along with the insults. To their credit, the soldiers obeyed the command to avoid fighting if possible and did not strike back at the young Bostonians.

One member of the Adams household bit the redcoats. The family had a huge dog named Queue, which they probably pro-nounced "Q." By this time Samuel Adams had decided to use only American and no English products in his home, so that "our oppressors may feel through their pockets the effects of their blind folly." Queue was a Newfoundland, a breed from Canada, which was near enough to the colonies to be acceptable to Samuel. Someone trained the 150-pound dog to bark and nip at the redcoats at every opportunity. It was said that the soldiers slashed at Queue with swords and shot at him, but that he had a charmed life despite being wounded several times.

Queue's master helped engineer a major political victory in early 1769. Samuel Adams had been calling for the removal of Governor Francis Bernard for a long time. His petitions and letters damaged Bernard's reputation in England, but something else hurt the governor even more. English merchants who were losing money because of the American boycott felt that Bernard

OPPOSITE: *"The Bostonians in Distress," an engraving made in England that seems to poke fun at both sides*

should have tried to make peace with the Bostonians. In the spring of 1769, Bernard was "recalled" to England, a polite way of firing him. After governing Massachusetts for nine years, Bernard was crestfallen to see how Bostonians celebrated on the summer day that he departed the colony. They fired cannons, chimed their church bells, and built a huge bonfire at Fort Hill not far from Samuel Adams's home.

Lieutenant Governor Thomas Hutchinson then became the acting governor of Massachusetts. A playwright could not have set the scene any better. Two men who deeply hated each other were about to engage in an epic clash with the future of a nation at stake.

CHAPTER V

The Street Fight That Became a "Massacre"

BEFORE THE BRITISH TROOPS ARRIVED in the fall of 1768, the cause of independence had been a passion with Samuel Adams. Now it became the focus of all his thoughts and deeds and the reason why he felt he had been born. "There was no pause" in Adams's efforts, wrote William Tudor, a Massachusetts lawmaker and author who knew him for many years. "Every day and every hour was employed in some contribution towards the main design [independence]. If not in action, in writing; if not with the pen, in conversation; if not in talking, in meditation."

Except for Sunday church, Betsy and the children saw little of him. Political meetings filled his days, while late into the night he wrote letters and articles for the *Boston Gazette*, the *Boston Evening Post*, and the *Boston News-Letter* under a variety of pseudonyms. John Adams later estimated that his cousin used up to a hundred pen names during his lifetime. A search of old Boston newspapers reveals that in 1769 alone he wrote under the names T. Z., Candidus, Shippen, E. A., a Layman, a Bostonian, a Tory, Populus, an Impartialist, Alfred, and a Son of Liberty. He also wrote petitions and appeals, countless personal letters to leaders throughout the thirteen colonies, and even an early American national anthem. Although the words and melody don't seem to fit, it was reportedly sung to the music now used for "My Country 'Tis of Thee":

The Liberty Song

Come join hand in hand, brave Americans all,
And rouse your bold hearts at fair Liberty's call;
No tyrannous acts shall suppress your just claim,
Or stain with dishonor America's name.

Our worthy forefathers, let's give 'em a cheer,
To climates unknown did courageously steer,
Thro' oceans to deserts for freedom they came,
And dying bequeath'd their freedom and fame.

How Samuel Adams supported his family starting around 1769 is a mystery. With his brewery closing that year, his only steady income was his small salary as clerk of the Massachusetts House of Representatives. According to gossip, the Adamses were so poor at this time that John Hancock and other friends sent them food to keep them from starving and repaired the Purchase Street house to keep it from falling. There was even a joke around Boston about Adams's letter writing: "Samuel Adams writes the letters and John Hancock pays the postage."

It was just a matter of time before the presence of the British troops was as explosive as Adams expected. One incident involved James Otis, who by this time was extremely disturbed, swinging between moods of joy and depression. On the night of September 5, 1769, Otis entered the British Coffee House on King Street. Apparently looking for trouble, Otis began arguing with the British officials, soldiers, and sailors who frequented the place. Suddenly the oil lamps were extinguished and Otis was attacked with swords. Blood pouring from his head, he had to be helped home by a passerby.

His injury seems to have pushed Otis into almost total insanity. His behavior became so bizarre that he was once found breaking the Old State House windows. The man who had spoken so eloquently about taxation without representation was tied up and taken out to the country to rest. Although he lived fourteen more years, James Otis was never again of much help to the patriots. In 1783 (the year America won its independence), the man John Adams had called "a flame of fire" as a public speaker dashed out of a house during a thunderstorm and was killed by lightning.

In early 1770, as the tension between Boston's rebels and Loyalists grew, a gang of boys painted pictures on a board making fun of merchants who still did business with England. On February 22, they set up the board and an IMPORTER sign in front of a merchant's house. Ebenezer Richardson, a Loyalist who lived nearby, tried to take down the board and sign, but the boys pelted him with rocks. Richardson ran home, opened his window, and fired his gun at the boys, severely wounding two of them. Twelve-year-old Christopher Snider died of his wounds.

Thomas Hutchinson sarcastically wrote, "The boy that was killed was the son of a poor German. A grand funeral was, however, judged very proper for him." Thousands of Bostonians joined the procession, which began at the Liberty Tree, passed the Old State House, and ended at the Granary Burial Ground.

Meanwhile, the mob broke into Richardson's house and carried him off to prison. He was charged with murder and found guilty, but Governor Thomas Hutchinson refused to sign the execution paper. After about two years, Richardson was released, pardoned by King George III.

A much more violent incident occurred a few days after the Christopher Snider shooting. Besides patrolling Boston, the British soldiers obtained part-time jobs, further angering the townspeople by depriving them of work. On March 2, 1770, a redcoat approached John Gray's Ropewalk (a rope-making business) seeking work. A rope maker named Sam Gray said that a job was available. When the soldier asked what kind, Gray answered, "You can clean out my shit-house!"

The soldier returned to his barracks and found some friends, who accompanied him back to the ropewalk. The rope makers were waiting with wooden clubs, which they used to beat up the redcoats that day as well as the next, when some soldiers again came to the ropewalk to fight. The two sides halted their battle on March 4 because it was a Sunday, but the soldiers vowed that the matter wasn't settled.

Snow fell on Monday, March 5. In the afternoon, the sky cleared, and by nightfall Boston looked peaceful beneath a first-quarter moon. The tranquil scene was deceiving. Groups of red-coats shoved and even struck townspeople they met on the streets, and many Bostonians also seemed to be spoiling for a fight. On King Street, a crowd composed partly of boys began taunting and throwing stones at a group of soldiers. When the troops were ordered back to their barracks to avoid trouble, the Bostonians turned on a redcoat guarding the British custom-house (a building where import taxes are paid) on King Street. They bombarded the man with snowballs, whistled through their fingers, and shouted, "The lobster dare not fire at us!"

"If you come near me, I will blow your brains out!" the terrified guard warned them. "Stand off!"

Meanwhile, a servant ran to the nearby barracks and reported, "They are killing the sentinel!"

Captain Thomas Preston rushed out with seven men, including one or two who had been thrashed at the ropewalk. As the red-coats loaded their muskets, the boys and men splattered them with snowballs while yelling insults. Suddenly a large object hit one of the soldiers, knocking him to the ground. Someone then shouted, "Fire!"—whether it was Captain Preston or a Bostonian daring the redcoats to shoot is unknown to this day. The next moment bullets were flying, and bodies were toppling and writhing in the blood-soaked snow.

When the shooting ended, three men lay dead: Crispus Attucks, thought to have been an escaped slave from an inland town; Sam Gray, the rope worker who had told the redcoat to clean his out-house; and James Caldwell, a sailor. Eight men were wounded, two fatally. Seventeen-year-old Samuel Maverick died the next morning. Patrick Carr, recently arrived from Ireland, clung to life for about a week before dying.

People told differing stories about the King Street brawl. The Loyalists claimed that the Bostonians had started it. They pointed to the testimony of Patrick Carr, who even as he lay dying from a British bullet admitted that the soldiers had fired in self-defense. Samuel Adams's followers claimed that the redcoats had used the throwing of a few snowballs and stones as an excuse to shoot down innocent people.

Samuel Adams knew that the Bostonians were hardly blameless, but he also realized that this was the chance he had awaited since the redcoats' arrival a year and a half earlier. Adams named the brawl the "Boston Massacre," and had his friend Paul Revere create an engraving of the event that backed up the patriots' version. So skillfully did Adams twist the truth that even today his portrayal of the Boston Massacre is the one nearly everyone believes.

At eleven o'clock on the morning after the Massacre, a huge town meeting assembled at Faneuil Hall. The townspeople decided that all the redcoats must leave Boston and appointed a committee of fifteen headed by Samuel Adams to inform the governor of this demand. Adams led the committee a short way to the Old

Paul Revere's famous engraving of the Boston Massacre. Samuel Adams had Revere make it look as though the redcoats ruthlessly shot down the helpless Americans.

The Boston Massacre

State House, where they were directed into the Council Chamber.

About thirty men, most of them the governor's councillors wearing scarlet coats and large white wigs, sat around a huge table. Governor Thomas Hutchinson, the most resplendent of them all, sat at the head of the table. Facing him was a forty-seven-year-old man with no wig covering his gray hair and probably no more than a few pennies in the pocket of his old red coat. In his quavering voice, Samuel Adams informed Governor Hutchinson of the town meeting's decision: All the troops must leave Boston.

He regretted the "unhappy differences," Hutchinson answered, but he could only send away the regiment involved in the violence. To remove the other soldiers would require an order from

The 29th Regiment have already left us, and the 14th Regiment are following them, so that we expect the Town will soon be clear of all the Troops. The Wisdom and true Policy of his Majesty's Council and Col. Dalrymple theCommander appear in this Measure. Two Regiments in the midst of this populous City; and the Inhabitants justly incensed: Those of the neighbouring Towns actually under Arms upon the first Report of the Massacre, and the Signal only wanting to bring in a few Hours to the Gates of this City many Thousands of our brave Brethren in the Country, deeply affected with our Distresses, and to whom we are greatly obliged on this Occasion—No one knows where this would have ended, and what important Consequences even to the whole British Empire might have followed, which our Moderation & Loyalty upon so trying anOccasion, and ourFaith in the Commander'sAssurances have happily prevented.

Last Thursday, agreeable to a general Request of the Inhabitants, and by the Consent of Parents and Friends, were carried to their *Graves* in Succession, the Bodies of *Samuel Gray, Samuel Maverick, James Caldwell,* and *Crispus Attucks,* the unhappy Victims who fell in the bloody Massacre of theMonday Evening preceeding!

On this Occasion most of the Shops in Town were shut, all the Bells were ordered to toll a solemn Peal, as were also those in the neighboring Towns of Charlestown Roxbury, &c. The Procession began to move between the Hours of 4 and 5 in the Afternoon; two of the unfortunate Sufferers, viz. Mess. *JamesCaldwell* and *Crispus Attucks,* who were Strangers, borne from Faneuil-Hall, attended by a numerous Train of Persons of all Ranks; and the other two, viz. Mr. *Samuel Gray,* from the House of Mr. Benjamin Gray, (his Brother) on the North-side the Exchange, and Mr. *Maverick,* from the House of his distressed Mother Mrs. *Mary Maverick,* in Union-Street, each followed by their respective Relations and Friends: The several Hearses forming a Junction in King-Street, the Theatre of that inhuman Tragedy! proceeded from thence thro' the Main-Street, lengthened by an immense Concourse of People, so numerous as to be obliged to follow in Ranks of six, and brought up by a long Train of Carriages belonging to the principal Gentry of theTown. The Bodies were deposited in one Vault in the middle Burying-ground: The aggravated Circumstances of their Death, the Distress and Sorrow visible in every Countenance, together with the peculiar Solemnity with which the whole Funeral was conducted, surpass Description.

This story appeared in the Boston Gazette *on March 12, 1770, a week after the Massacre. Paul Revere did the engravings of the coffins. The initials stand for Sam Gray, Samuel Maverick, James Caldwell, and Crispus Attucks. Patrick Carr died after Revere did the engraving.*

General Thomas Gage, commander in chief of British forces in North America. Since Gage's headquarters were in New York City, this would take time.

Upon his return to Faneuil Hall with Hutchinson's response, Adams found that three thousand people had gathered—more than the place could hold. The crowd poured through the streets to the Old South Meeting House, but this church could not admit everyone, either. About half the crowd had to wait outside while Samuel Adams read Hutchinson's reply to those inside the building. When he finished, Adams told the townspeople that he found the governor's answer unacceptable and asked if they found it satisfactory. Only one voice yelled "Aye!" while the rest shouted "No!"

Adams and his committee then

The Old South Church, where the huge meeting was held the day after the Massacre

walked back to the Old State House to meet with Governor Hutchinson once more. It was now late afternoon, and the sky had begun to darken. Candles flickered off the faces of the two enemies as Samuel Adams explained the town's decision. "It is the unanimous opinion of the meeting," said Adams, apparently forgetting the one person who disagreed, "that the reply to the vote of the inhabitants is by no means satisfactory. Nothing less will satisfy them than a total and immediate removal of the troops!"

"The troops are not subject to my authority," insisted Hutchinson. "I have no power to remove them."

Anger flashing in his eyes, Samuel Adams pointed his finger at the governor and said: "If you have the power to remove one regiment, you have power to remove both. It is at your peril if you refuse. The meeting is composed of three thousand people. They have become impatient. The whole country is in motion. Night is approaching. An immediate answer is expected. Both regiments or none!"

Hutchinson turned to his councillors for advice. One of them warned: "The people will come in from the neighboring towns. There will be ten thousand men to effect the removal of the troops, be the consequence what it may!" In a letter to a friend about this famous confrontation, Samuel Adams wrote that Hutchinson's face turned pale and his knees trembled as he considered his options. Finally, the governor reached a decision. He backed down and gave the order for both regiments to be removed.

Samuel Adams is the picture of determination in the portrait (shown on the cover of this book) that John Singleton Copley painted of him arguing with Hutchinson about the troops. Inwardly, though, Adams was as worried as Hutchinson when the two men faced off late that afternoon of March 6, 1770. Massachusetts might be able to raise enough men to drive all the redcoats out of Boston, Adams knew. But he also realized that people in other colonies were not yet ready for war and would not help when tens of thousands of redcoats were sent to Massachusetts to crush the revolt. So when he returned to the Old South Meeting House and told the cheering throng the great news, Adams was probably the most relieved person in Boston.

A few days later, a crowd gathered to watch the redcoats march down King Street, much as they had watched them march up that same street a year and a half earlier. Some Sons of Liberty paraded alongside the soldiers to mock them, and children yelled "Good-bye, bloody lobsters!" as the soldiers approached the wharf. When British prime minister Lord Frederick North heard

"Both regiments or none!" Samuel Adams warned Governor Thomas Hutchinson. This picture is one of several that other artists created based on the famous portrait by John Singleton Copley shown on the cover.

how Samuel Adams had forced (actually bluffed) Hutchinson into backing down, he called the departed troops "the Sam Adams regiments"—a nickname that was in wide use for many years. Lord North became so convinced that Adams was responsible for the growing rebellion that he began to refer to all the American patriots as "Adams's crew." For the same reason, a number of Loyalists began to refer to the troubles in the thirteen colonies as "Adams's conspiracy."

The departure of the troops was one victory, but to most Bostonians the scales of justice would not be balanced until Captain Thomas Preston and the seven other soldiers were executed for perpetrating the Massacre. The defendants had difficulty obtaining a lawyer. Samuel Adams shocked people when he arranged for his friends John Adams and Josiah Quincy—two of Boston's leading lawyers—to defend the men. One possible explanation is that Quincy and the Adams cousins assumed the redcoats would be sentenced to death no matter who defended them. If the soldiers were provided with the finest lawyers, the world would see that Bostonians were a fair-minded people who valued justice over vengeance.

Once the trial began in the fall of 1770, John Adams and Josiah Quincy did such a good job that not one of the eight redcoats was hanged. The jury found six of them not guilty. Two were found guilty of manslaughter, a lesser charge than murder, and were sentenced to be branded on the thumb with a hot iron.

Samuel Adams found two sources of consolation in the outcome. The Bostonians had proved that even British soldiers could receive a fair trial in their town. Also, since most Americans felt that the redcoats had gotten away with murder, Adams could use the verdict to his advantage whenever resistance to England began to slip. Much as the phrase "Remember the Alamo!" became a war cry during Texas's fight for independence from Mexico in the 1830s, Adams in the 1770s would continually remind the colonists to "Remember the bloody Massacre!" With Samuel Adams doing the reminding, how could they possibly forget?

CHAPTER VI

The Harbor That Became a "Teapot"

LIKE THE STAMP ACT BEFORE THEM, the Townshend Acts failed to bring in the funds the British expected; the American boycott of British goods also proved costly. By 1770 many English people wanted to repeal the Townshend Acts and restore friendly relations with the colonists. To King George III and most members of Parliament, however, taxes were no longer the main issue in the conflict. They viewed the Americans as rebellious children who must obey their mother country. On March 5, 1770—the day of the Boston Massacre—Parliament repealed all the Townshend Acts except the tax on tea. That alone would preserve the principle that England could impose its will on the colonists.

Samuel Adams explained that one tax was as evil as ten and still violated the principle of taxation without representation. But most Americans viewed the repeal as a victory, and for about three years they were little disturbed by the tax on tea, especially since Dutch tea was smuggled in for those who had a thirst for the popular drink. Even in Boston, America's most rebellious city,

THE HORSE AMERICA, *throwing his Master.*

Most people in England were disturbed by the Americans' rebelliousness. America (the horse) is throwing off English rule (the rider, King George III) in this English engraving.

people were weary of the arguing and street fighting, and did not seem to mind a little injustice. By mid-1770 the other colonies had for the most part ended their boycott of British goods, and most Bostonians wanted to follow suit. Boston must fight on alone, if need be, Adams told the town's merchants, but they stunned him by voting 68 to 5 to end the boycott.

To many Bostonians, Samuel Adams had become a walking relic—a reminder of the noble fight against the Stamp Act, but a man out of step with the times. He still sent letters to other colonial leaders, but now when he wrote that he had "long feared this unhappy contest between Great Britain and America would end in rivers of blood," it sounded melodramatic. He still sent essays to newspapers, but they were often rejected. When Adams scheduled ceremonies at the Liberty Tree, only a handful of people showed up, and when he called for meetings at Faneuil Hall to discuss British injustice, there were times when fewer than a hundred people attended.

Adams had entered a period when nothing seemed to go right. He lost squabbles to Thomas Hutchinson, who was widely praised in Massachusetts for avoiding war despite a steady stream of abuse. Samuel grew angry at his cousin for not opposing the mother country as firmly as he did, and he had a serious split with John Hancock in 1770 that lasted two years. No one but Samuel Adams and John Hancock knew the cause of their feud, and they didn't talk about it, but there are several theories. Hancock may have grown tired of the Loyalists' claim that he was Adams's puppet. Adams may have discovered that Hancock was thinking of switching to the Loyalist side. Perhaps Hancock finally understood that Adams wanted independence, a bold step the merchant was not ready to take. Or perhaps Hancock's feelings were hurt when he realized that Samuel Adams preferred his money to his friendship.

Samuel was philosophical about his loss of popularity. He even said to his teenage daughter, Hannah, who remembered the comment years later: "I am in fashion and out of fashion, as the whim goes. I will stand alone!" Adams also knew that the "spark of patriotic fire" might be burning low, but that one nudge from England and it would burst into flame again. Until then, he would write articles for whatever newspapers would print them and hold protest meetings even if only one person attended.

Adams's lowest point during the revolutionary era occurred in the spring of 1772, when his enemies tried to deny him reelection to the Massachusetts House. He won, but with a lower percentage of votes than usual. Things improved after that. He and John Hancock ended their quarrel, possibly because the merchant decided that he stood firm with the Liberty Party and would place the cause before his personal feelings. Hancock loved happy occasions. To celebrate the return of cordial relations between Samuel Adams and himself, he hired his Beacon Hill neighbor John Singleton Copley to paint their portraits. This was when Copley created the portrait of Adams facing Governor Hutchinson. The portraits of Hancock and Adams hung side by side in Hancock's parlor for fifty years, and today are in the collection of Boston's Museum of Fine Arts.

Near the end of this quiet period, Adams made one of his greatest contributions to his country. On November 2, 1772, at a town meeting in Faneuil Hall, he stood up and said: "I move that a Committee of Correspondence be appointed, to consist of twenty-one persons, to state the rights of the colonists and of this province in particular, and to communicate and publish the same to the world." The townspeople approved the idea that day, marking the birth of America's first official Committee of Correspondence. Similar committees soon sprang up across America in imitation of Boston's, and soon these letter-writing networks had a much more serious matter to discuss than governors' salaries and multiple officeholding.

In May 1773, Parliament passed the Tea Act, which cut the price of tea almost in half while maintaining the tax on it. British lawmakers felt that the new law was a stroke of genius because it would accomplish three goals. It would lure the Americans into buying tea from a huge English firm called the East India Company, reduce the colonists' smuggling of Dutch tea, and demonstrate that saving money meant more to them than their taxation without representation argument.

The strategy failed, because the Americans weren't as simple-minded or as greedy as Parliament thought. Instead of enticing the Americans into paying the tax on tea, the new law ignited a firestorm of anger. Suddenly it was like 1765 again, with protest meetings under Liberty Trees, defiant newspaper articles, and talk in every tavern about how England was trying to fool the colonists. Women and girls also became involved, which was remarkable in an age when females were expected to stay out of politics. They formed groups called the Daughters of Liberty and signed pledges that they would not purchase English tea. Instead they brewed homemade tea for their families out of raspberries, mint leaves, or sassafras roots and called it "liberty tea."

With the passage of the Tea Act, a man in a faded red suit suddenly became more "in fashion" than ever before. Bostonians boasted: Who had warned Americans that the principle of taxation, not the amount of the tax, was what mattered? Who had begun the Committees of Correspondence that would help colonial leaders plan unified action? Their own Samuel Adams—that was who!

Perhaps it was at this time that Adams was nicknamed the Prophet Samuel because he seemed to have the ability to gaze into the future. Samuel's great-grandson William V. Wells wrote that some Bostonians began to think that "he was actually gifted with prophecy, and not a few believed that he held peace or war in his keeping."

Word reached America in the fall of 1773 that ships bearing British tea would arrive in Boston by late November. The tea was to be consigned to agents who would then sell it. On November 1, 1773—exactly eight years after the Stamp Act was supposed to take effect—messages were posted on the doors of Boston's tea agents, who included two sons of Governor Thomas Hutchinson. The tea agents were ordered to appear at the Liberty Tree at noon of November 3 to publicly resign their positions. These messages were probably written according to Samuel Adams's instructions, as was the following notice that was posted around Boston:

Artists of the eighteenth and nineteenth centuries often copied one another's work, which today is considered dishonest. Compare this picture showing protests against the Stamp and Tea Acts to the one (page 31) of an earlier date. The artist just reversed the image and made a few other changes.

Gentlemen,—You are desired to meet at the Liberty Tree this day at twelve o'clock at noon, then and there to hear the persons to whom the tea shipped by the East India Company is consigned make a public resignation of their offices as consignees upon oath; and also swear that they will reship any teas that may be consigned to them by the said Company, by the first sailing vessel to London.

Boston, November 3, 1773

☞ Show me the man that dare take this down!

On the morning of November 3, a crowd of up to a thousand people gathered at the Liberty Tree. They cheered when Samuel Adams and John Hancock arrived. However, Boston's church bells chimed the noon hour and the tea agents did not appear. A committee was sent to the warehouse where they were hiding, but the agents refused to sign a pledge stating that they would reship the tea to England.

Over the next few weeks there were further attempts to force the agents to resign, and messages were sent to Governor Hutchinson asking that he not allow the tea into Boston. All these efforts failed, as Samuel Adams had hoped, for it meant that the Sons of Liberty could carry out his secret plan for a "tea party."

The first of the tea ships, the *Dartmouth*, arrived in Boston Harbor on November 28, followed soon after by the *Eleanor* and the *Beaver*. The Sons of Liberty posted armed guards at Griffin's Wharf to watch over the three ships and make sure that the agents did not try to sneak the tea ashore. Meanwhile, Samuel Adams was whipping the patriots into a frenzy, as demonstrated by a message that he sent to towns near Boston in late November:

> Now brethren, we are reduced to this dilemma, either to sit down quiet under this and every other burden that our enemies shall see fit to lay upon us as good-natured slaves, or rise and resist this and every other plan laid for our destruction, as becomes wise freemen. In this extremity we earnestly request your advice, and that you would give us the earliest intelligence of the sense your several towns have of the present gloomy situation of our affairs.

By mid-December Adams had completed the details of his secret plan. On Thursday, December 16, the largest public gathering Boston had ever held in its 143-year history took place at the Old South Meeting House. About five thousand Bostonians and two thousand people from outlying areas crowded into and around the church. Since Boston's population was about seventeen thousand, nearly every adult in the Massachusetts capital must have attended this gigantic town meeting.

The townspeople decided to send a final request asking that Hutchinson send away the tea ships. As they awaited the governor's answer, people in the meeting house stood up and made defiant speeches. One man hinted at what was coming by saying:

"Who knows how tea will mingle with salt water?" His comment drew loud applause. Finally, at about six at night, the messenger returned with the response that Samuel Adams and nearly everyone else had expected: Hutchinson absolutely refused to send the ships back to England.

Samuel Adams then arose and faced the multitude of angry Bostonians. "This meeting can do nothing more to save the country!" he shouted. These words were a prearranged signal to forty or fifty men, disguised as Indians, who were posted at the church entrance.

"Boston Harbor a teapot tonight!" whooped the "Indians," waving their hatchets. The war party set off along Milk Street toward Griffin's Wharf. As the crowd emptied out of the Old South, John Hancock was heard to say, "Let every man do what is right in his own eyes!" Many in the crowd decided to help the "Indians" dispose of the tea, for by this time everyone knew the purpose of the hatchets.

Not counting spectators, the mob contained about a hundred and fifty people by the time it reached Griffin's Wharf. Most of their identities remain unknown, but we do know that Paul Revere was among them. By the light of torches and lanterns, the men boarded the three ships, smashed open the 342 chests (some sources say 340) with their hatchets, then dumped all the tea into Boston Harbor.

Their mission accomplished, the Bostonians marched home to the tooting of a fife. As the men joked about having turned Boston Harbor into a "teapot," Admiral John Montagu of the British Navy stuck his head out a window and said, "Well, boys, you've had a fine, pleasant evening for your Indian caper. But mind, he who dances must pay the fiddler." A leader of the tea party shouted back, "Oh, never mind, Admiral. Just come out here, if you please, and we'll settle the bill in two minutes!"

The Boston Tea Party, one of the most famous events in United States history

Most Bostonians considered the destruction of the tea a brave and necessary act of defiance. Even John Adams, who loathed violence and destruction, said that the Boston Tea Party was "the most magnificent act" the patriots had yet perpetrated. But no one was happier than Samuel Adams, who on New Year's Eve of 1773 wrote a letter to a friend about the events of December 16. "You cannot imagine the height of joy that sparkles in the eyes and animates the [faces] as well as the hearts of all [Bostonians]," he wrote. Also on December 31, the *Boston Gazette* printed a New Year's message from Samuel Adams charged with the highly emotional style he was using to move his fellow Americans closer to war:

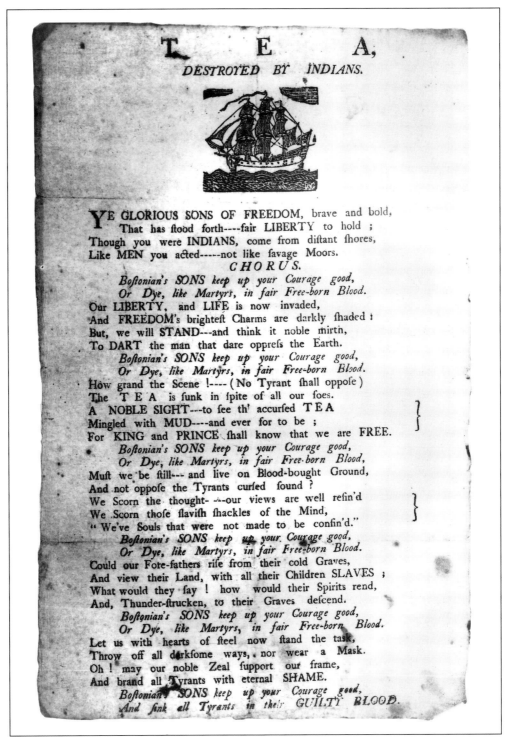

T E A,

DESTROYED BY INDIANS.

YE GLORIOUS SONS OF FREEDOM, brave and bold,
That has stood forth----fair LIBERTY to hold ;
Though you were INDIANS, come from distant shores,
Like MEN you acted-----not like savage Moors.

CHORUS.

Bostonian's SONS keep up your Courage good,
Or Dye, like Martyrs, in fair Free-born Blood.

Our LIBERTY, and LIFE is now invaded,
And FREEDOM's brightest Charms are darkly shaded :
But, we will STAND---and think it noble mirth,
To DART the man that dare oppress the Earth.

Bostonian's SONS keep up your Courage good,
Or Dye, like Martyrs, in fair Free-born Blood.

How grand the Scene !----(No Tyrant shall oppose)
The T E A is sunk in spite of all our foes.
A NOBLE SIGHT---to see th' accursed T E A
Mingled with MUD----and ever for to be ;
For KING and PRINCE shall know that we are FREE.

Bostonian's SONS keep up your Courage good,
Or Dye, like Martyrs, in fair Free-born Blood,

Must we be still--- and live on Blood-bought Ground,
And not oppose the Tyrants cursed found ?
We Scorn the thought- --our views are well refin'd
We Scorn those slavish shackles of the Mind,
" We've Souls that were not made to be confin'd."

Bostonian's SONS keep up your Courage good,
Or Dye, like Martyrs, in fair Free-born Blood.

Could our Fore-fathers rise from their cold Graves,
And view their Land, with all their Children SLAVES ;
What would they say ! how would their Spirits rend,
And, Thunder-strucken, to their Graves descend.

Bostonian's SONS keep up your Courage good,
Or Dye, like Martyrs, in fair Free-born Blood.

Let us with hearts of steel now stand the task,
Throw off all darksome ways, nor wear a Mask.
Oh ! may our noble Zeal support our frame,
And brand all Tyrants with eternal SHAME.

Bostonian's SONS keep up your Courage good,
And sink all Tyrants in their GUILTY BLOOD.

Some patriot composed this song about the Boston Tea Party. Perhaps Samuel Adams had a hand in writing it.

To all Nations under Heaven, know ye, that the PEOPLE of the AMERICAN WORLD are Millions strong—countless Legions compose their ARMY OF FREEMEN. . . . AMERICA now stands with the Scale of JUSTICE in one Hand, and the Sword of VENGEANCE in the other. . . . Let the Britons fear to do any more so wickedly as they have done, for the HERCULEAN ARM of this NEW WORLD is lifted up—and Woe be to them on whom it falls!—At the Beat of the Drum, she can call five Hundred Thousand of her SONS to ARMS. . . .Therefore, ye that are wise, make Peace with her, take Shelter under her Wings, that ye may shine by the Reflection of her Glory.

May the NEW YEAR shine propitious on the NEW WORLD—and VIRTUE and LIBERTY reign here without a Foe, until rolling Years shall measure Time no more.

A 1774 almanac cover showing Governor Thomas Hutchinson with two evil characters, implying that he is the devil's tool. Isaiah Thomas, a Boston printer known for his anti-British views, published the almanac. Twelve years later, in 1786, Thomas would publish the first Mother Goose *book known to have been printed in America.*

CHAPTER VII

"The Common Cause of America"

$\mathcal{I}$F SAMUEL ADAMS MADE A NEW YEAR'S WISH as the city's church bells rang in the year 1774, it may have been for other colonies to imitate the Boston Tea Party. This was precisely what happened, as many towns, including New York City and Annapolis, Maryland, held tea parties in 1774. Although outraged by each new act of destruction, the British were especially disturbed by the original Tea Party, because they knew who had been the instigator yet they couldn't prove it. Not until the end of the Revolutionary War did participants admit that Samuel Adams had orchestrated the Boston Tea Party. But not even in his old age, when every schoolchild knew about it, would Adams discuss his role in the event. He wanted Americans to think of the Tea Party as a massive and almost spontaneous rebellion by the people of Boston, which is exactly how it is remembered today. An interesting sidelight to the Tea Party is that it helped make the name *Boston* synonymous with rebellion. Fifty years later, English traders three thousand miles to the west of Massachusetts were still warning Pacific Coast Indians to stay away from the troublemaking "Bostons," meaning the Americans, and to trade with the English "King George men" instead.

British lawmakers had already backed down from the Americans twice—during the troubles with the Stamp Act and the Townshend Acts. They were not about to retreat a third time, for they feared that this would only invite further rebellion. In the spring of 1774, Parliament voted to punish Boston, in the form of what became known to the colonists as the Intolerable Acts. Starting June 1, no ships would be allowed in or out of Boston Harbor until the townspeople paid for the tea. Since Boston was a major seaport, this would cost many people their jobs and perhaps even result in large-scale starvation. Also, Massachusetts was to be placed under the command of General Thomas Gage, a military governor with a large army behind him. To make things worse, the colonists were required to feed and house Gage's soldiers, and town meetings without the governor's permission were to be outlawed.

Not yet aware of these acts, the Bostonians continued to flex their muscles. Each year on or near March 5, they assembled for a patriotic speech to remember the Massacre victims and renew their hatred for British oppression. John Hancock was named speaker for the fourth anniversary in 1774 and proudly accepted the honor before realizing that he had no talent for speechwriting. Samuel Adams refused to lose this opportunity for deepening Hancock's involvement in the cause, so he wrote a speech for him. Hannah Adams later said that her father and Hancock met several times to rehearse the speech, but that she was warned to keep this secret. At the time, it was considered dishonest for one person to write a speech for another.

On March 5, a huge crowd assembled at the Old South Meeting House to hear Hancock. He proved to be a far more brilliant and fiery speaker than anyone had expected. Hancock went so far as to suggest that perhaps the colonists should free themselves from

Great Britain and form a new country called the United States of America—one of the first times this name was proposed.

News of the Intolerable Acts reached Boston two months after Hancock's stirring speech. Boston's Committee of Correspondence immediately invited leaders from several neighboring towns to a convention that was held May 12 in the Massachusetts capital. Despite the hardships this would cause, the convention decided that Boston should not pay for the tea.

Samuel Adams had always tried to involve as many people as possible in his crusade—even crediting others for his own deeds—so that the independence movement would grow. Now he began a campaign to convince all thirteen colonies that England's punishment of Boston was a blow to all of them. Boston was "suffering in the common cause of America," he explained in letters that Paul Revere and other riders delivered to leaders throughout the colonies.

General Thomas Gage sailed into Boston Harbor on May 13. Any joy the Bostonians felt when Thomas Hutchinson left America a few days later was canceled by their worry over the new governor's arrival. Gage was a popular and friendly man who had lived in the American colonies for many years and had married a New Jersey woman. However, he hadn't become commander in chief of Great Britain's North American forces by letting his heart rule his head. Everyone in Boston knew that he had come to do a job, which was to crush the rebellion before it grew any stronger.

By 1774 the British were convinced that, as historian James Hosmer wrote, "Massachusetts led the thirteen colonies, Boston led Massachusetts, and Samuel Adams led Boston." That spring and summer, rumors swept the city that Samuel Adams and John Hancock were about to be arrested and hanged for treason, for King George III himself had warned Gage that he wanted "the principal ringleaders" of the Boston Tea Party punished as an

General Thomas Gage, who had an uncanny resemblance to Samuel Adams

"example to others." The Loyalists gleefully anticipated the double execution. Admiral John Montagu, who had spoken of paying the fiddler the night of the Tea Party, wrote in 1774: "I doubt not but that I shall hear Mr. Samuel Adams is hanged or shot before many months are at an end. I hope so at least." Boston's Loyalists also began chanting a little ditty:

> *As for their King, that John Hancock,*
> *And Adams, if they're taken;*
> *Their heads for signs shall hang up high*
> *Upon the hill called Beacon!*

The patriots were so worried that Gage would have Adams pulled from his bed that they placed bars on the doors and windows of his Purchase Street house. However, these were little protection against the five thousand redcoats who had reached Boston within a short time of Gage's arrival.

Samuel Adams's bravery and calmness during this period amazed the patriots and frustrated the Loyalists. He continued to organize resistance and walk the streets, even taking John Adams's seven-year-old son John Quincy Adams out onto Boston Common to watch the redcoats drill. Perhaps Samuel Adams was so tranquil because he trusted that the Sons of Liberty would keep his role in the Tea Party secret. It is also possible that he *hoped* the British would arrest and execute him, for he would have gladly given his life if it would inspire others to fight for America's freedom.

Gradually, the good news for which Adams had been praying reached Boston. The other colonies considered Boston to be "suffering in the common cause" and vowed to stand shoulder to shoulder with the town. On June 1—the day Boston's port was first shut down—patriots in Philadelphia, Pennsylvania, closed their businesses for the day and tolled their church bells mournfully. In Virginia, the legislature followed Thomas Jefferson's advice and spent the day in prayer and fasting.

The port closure caused great hardship in Boston. Goods and food couldn't be shipped in, so business dwindled throughout the city and thousands of Bostonians faced the threat of famine. But instead of giving in to the pressure, most Bostonians were so incensed over the Intolerable Acts that they were ready to eat shoe leather rather than pay for the tea. Fortunately this wasn't necessary, because other colonies rushed to Boston's aid.

Nearby towns such as Salem and Marblehead, Massachusetts, allowed Boston to use their ports. Food was shipped to these towns, then carted overland to Boston. Patriots in Rhode Island, New York, Maryland, North and South Carolina, and other colonies sent in corn, rye, beef, fish, sugar, bread, pork, rice, and money.

The most unusual donation was a flock of 130 sheep that Israel Putnam, a hero of the French and Indian War, led about a hundred miles from Connecticut to Boston. Samuel Adams was chairman of the donation committee that passed out food to the needy.

The Bostonians evaded the ban on town meetings by calling the gatherings by a different name. The whole town might attend a donation committee meeting, in effect turning it into a town meeting. At one such meeting in 1774, Adams listened to the townspeople's usual complaints about the British and then arose to tell a story. "A philosopher, who was asleep upon the grass, was aroused by the bite of some animal upon the palm of his hand," Adams began. "He closed his hand as he awoke, and found that he had caught a field mouse, which bit him a second time. He dropped it, and it made its escape. Now, fellow citizens, what think you was the reflection he made upon this circumstance?" He waited a few seconds, then answered his own question. "It was this: that there is no animal, however weak, which cannot defend its own liberty, if it will only *fight* for it!"

For a long time, Samuel Adams had wanted to form a congress composed of representatives from all thirteen colonies. Historians credit Adams and Benjamin Franklin with independently originating this idea in 1773. After the Intolerable Acts took effect, colonial leaders realized that the time had come to follow Adams's and Franklin's suggestion. The First Continental Congress, as it came to be known, was scheduled for September 1774 in Philadelphia. In the weeks before the convention, the colonies selected their delegates.

Soon after his arrival, Governor Thomas Gage had moved the Massachusetts capital twenty miles northeast to Salem, in the hope that the Boston radicals would have less influence there. Samuel Adams and the Liberty Party decided that the House of Representatives would select the colony's delegates to Congress on June 17. They kept this secret, for if Gage knew about it, he would try to stop them from voting for the delegates.

When Samuel Adams entered the temporary capitol building in Salem on June 17, John Hancock told him there were eleven Loyalist legislators present, any of whom might run out and inform Gage about the upcoming vote. To prevent this, Adams locked the door and told the guard not to let anyone in or out while the meeting was in session. The House then voted 120 to 11 to send delegates to the Continental Congress and elected the Adams cousins, Thomas Cushing (son of the man at whose countinghouse Samuel had worked), James Bowdoin, and Robert Treat Paine to represent the colony. John Hancock was not chosen because Samuel Adams had an important assignment for him at home in Massachusetts.

During the deliberations, one of the eleven Loyalists told the watchman that he felt ill and needed to leave the hall. The guard believed him and opened the door. Once outside the building, the Loyalist galloped off to the governor. Gage sent his secretary to

Thomas Cushing, the son of the man who had employed Samuel Adams at his counting- house many years earlier

order the House dissolved, but the lawmakers refused to open the door until their business was finished. When they adjourned that day, it proved to be the last time the Massachusetts House met as a colonial body.

Samuel Adams's friends realized that there was a practical problem with his attending the convention. He had no decent clothes. The Massachusetts patriots didn't want the rest of the country to think they were led by a pauper (which they were), so they concocted a scheme.

One summer evening, Adams and his family were eating supper when there was a knock at their door. Samuel was surprised to find that a well-known tailor had come to visit. He asked to take Adams's measurements, but refused to say who had sent him. The Adamses had returned to their meal when there was a second rap at the door. This time it was a popular hat maker. As he measured Samuel's head, he, too, refused to tell who had sent him. Next came a shoemaker, a wig maker, and several other shopkeepers, but none would answer Samuel's question.

A few days later, a large trunk was delivered to the Adams home. Inside it, Samuel found a brand-new wardrobe that included a handsome suit, two pairs of shoes, a cocked hat, a wig, a gold-handled cane, and a red (his favorite color) cloak. The cane and the sleeve buttons on the suit bore liberty-cap emblems. Since this cone-shaped cap was the symbol of the Sons of Liberty, many people thought that they had sent the gifts. It was also said that, in addition to the clothing, Adams was given a coin-filled purse.

James Bowdoin could not attend the Continental Congress because his wife was ill. The four who were bound for Philadelphia gathered at Thomas Cushing's house on August 10 along with friends and relatives who came to see them off. Betsy Adams was there with Samuel's children, now both grown. Twenty-three-year-old Samuel had studied medicine with his father's friend Dr. Joseph Warren and had become a physician.

Hannah, eighteen, would be married in a few years. Abigail Adams, John's wife, was there, too, dressed in a white bonnet and flowery summer dress that matched Betsy's outfit. Also on hand were John Hancock and his beautiful lady friend, Dolly Quincy, who for several years had been refusing his marriage proposals. Surrounded by all these elegant people, Samuel Adams was the center of attention. Seeing him in fine clothing, his friends and relatives realized something that his tatters had hidden: Samuel was actually a handsome man!

There were many moist eyes at the farewell, for in the eighteenth century people commonly became ill and died on long journeys. Toasts were drunk to the Sons of Liberty and to the Continental Congress, and then, after some final good-byes, the delegates climbed into their coach and were off. Four armed guards rode alongside the vehicle in case the British tried to arrest the delegates.

As the coach rolled southwest toward Philadelphia, Samuel Adams was probably the most excited of the four delegates. At fifty-one, he was about to leave Massachusetts for the first time ever. More important, his dream of a Continental Congress was about to be realized, and he would soon be shaking the hands of men with whom he had corresponded for years.

Every town in Massachusetts had pitched in to pay the delegates' expenses. There were no hotels in those days, so the travelers stopped at taverns, which provided them with food, drink, and a place to sleep. Word spread of their passing, and patriots on horseback approached their carriage and accompanied them for a while along the way. On August 29, the Massachusetts delegates reached Philadelphia, "dirty, dusty, and fatigued" according to John Adams. Today the three hundred miles between Boston and Philadelphia can be driven by car in about six hours, but the delegates had taken nineteen days to complete the journey. The four men rented a house in Philadelphia for their lodgings.

The First Continental Congress, which was a forerunner to our U.S. Congress, opened in Carpenters' Hall on September 5, 1774. Georgia, the home of many Loyalists, sent no delegates, but the other twelve colonies sent a total of fifty-six representatives. Leaders from various regions were eager to meet one another for the first time. The delicate manners and drawling accents of Virginian George Washington and other southern planters intrigued the New Englanders. The New England twang of the Massachusetts, Connecticut, New Hampshire, and Rhode Island men amused the southerners. Samuel Adams must have been especially interested to meet several men who had been nick-named for him because of their zeal for the cause: Christopher Gadsden, the "Samuel Adams of South Carolina," Samuel Chase, the "Samuel Adams of Maryland," and convention secretary Charles Thomson, the "Samuel Adams of Philadelphia." Adams would have liked to have met Cornelius Harnett, but the "Samuel Adams of North Carolina" was not yet appointed to Congress, so that had to wait for another day.

Once the convention got down to business, a mood of uncer-tainty and fear set in. The delegates agreed that England must stop taxing America and punishing Boston for its Tea Party, but they weren't sure how to achieve this. If they didn't assert them-selves, Parliament would ignore them. Yet if they were too bold in demanding reforms, the mother country might retaliate against all the colonies. Something else worried nearly everyone in Carpenters' Hall. Two delegates—Samuel Adams and Patrick Henry—were known to favor independence from England. The mother country considered the thirteen colonies the jewels of its possessions and would fight to keep them. A war against the world's strongest nation was as terrifying a prospect as most of the representatives could imagine.

OPPOSITE: *Artist's version of the delegates leaving Carpenters' Hall after a session of the First Continental Congress*

Adams realized that his ideas troubled the great majority of his fellow congressmen. Under his direction, the Massachusetts delegation decided to let other colonies take the lead in Congress while working quietly behind the scenes. Samuel even served in the unlikely role of peacemaker as the proceedings began. Probably at his bidding, Thomas Cushing suggested that a minister open the convention with a prayer. Quite a few of the delegates were Episcopalians and wanted the Reverend Jacob Duché to deliver the prayer, but members of other faiths preferred someone of their own denomination. Most of the New England delegates, including Samuel Adams, were Congregationalists, as the Puritans had become known, and there were also Quakers, Baptists, Presbyterians, and Unitarians in Congress. John Jay of New York spoke for the majority when he told Cushing that they were too divided over religion to worship together.

Samuel Adams then rose to speak. Sometimes called the "Last of the Puritans" because he was so strict in his beliefs that he seemed to be a throwback to Boston's founders, Adams was the last man his fellow delegates expected to speak on behalf of an Episcopalian minister. But Adams seemed to have set up this scene just so that he could foster a spirit of cooperation in Congress. "I hope I am not a bigot, and can hear a prayer from a gentleman of piety and virtue who is a friend to his country," he said. "I am a stranger in Philadelphia, but I have heard that Mr. Duché deserves that character. Therefore I move that Mr. Duché be asked to read prayers to the Congress." Suddenly the other delegates were ashamed over their bickering. Duché led the first prayer in Congress, which became the subject of numerous paintings and poems. Adams's ploy helped unify the convention and may have even changed the course of U. S. history.

Joseph Galloway, a Philadelphia lawyer who wanted to reconcile with the mother country, proposed a plan by which British rule would continue with some changes. For example, the colonists would have a president-general appointed by the king and would gain limited control over their affairs through a national legislature. Had Galloway's plan been approved, the thirteen colonies might have remained part of the British Empire indefinitely. Fortunately for the cause of American independence, the plan was defeated by the narrowest margin—*one* vote. Galloway bitterly placed the blame for the defeat on Samuel Adams, and later described how Adams influenced Congress while at the same time directing events back in Boston:

> Continued expresses [messengers on horseback] were employed between Philadelphia and Boston. These were under the management of Samuel Adams—a man who . . . eats little, drinks little, sleeps little, thinks much, and is most decisive and indefatigable in the pursuit of his objects. It was this man, who, by his superior application, managed at once the faction in Congress at Philadelphia and the factions in New England. . . .

Patrick Henry was the delegate most in accord with Samuel Adams's opinions. Henry's speech on the second day was one of the most electrifying events of the convention. "The distinctions between Virginians, Pennsylvanians, New Yorkers, and New Englanders are no more!" cried the Son of Thunder. "I am not a Virginian, but an American!" This was precisely what Samuel Adams meant when he spoke of "the common cause of America," but Henry's was a far more eloquent way to say it.

The First Continental Congress wasn't nearly as radical as Samuel Adams had hoped, but through his talking to delegates behind the scenes and Patrick Henry stirring them through his speeches, the convention moved the country a little closer to independence. For one thing, Congress sent word to all thirteen colonies that their emergency troops, known as *militias*, must be armed and ready for action. Congress also passed a resolution calling for a new boycott of British goods. Starting December 1, 1774, Americans weren't to buy any British products. Beginning September 10, 1775, nearly all shipments of American goods to England were to be cut off. In addition, the congressmen drew up petitions demanding justice and sent them to England. Before adjourning on October 26, 1774, Congress decided to assemble again in Philadelphia in the spring if British lawmakers refused their demands.

Two days after the seven-week convention ended, the Massachusetts delegates left Philadelphia. After a twelve-day journey, they entered Boston the evening of November 9 to the ringing of bells and the cheering of crowds.

Joseph Galloway's assessment was accurate. Samuel Adams *had* managed affairs at home by writing letters from Philadelphia. After selecting its delegates to Congress, the Massachusetts colonial legislature had not met again. In early October, Massachusetts lawmakers in Salem followed Adams's advice and formed a new legislature, the Provincial Congress, which was the start of the Massachusetts state government. John Hancock was chosen as the chairman of this temporary government (which was why Samuel had wanted him to remain at home), and Adams was elected as a delegate while in Philadelphia.

The Massachusetts Provincial Congress told each town to prepare its militia for battle. Across the colony, units began drilling on village greens. About a third of the Massachusetts troops called themselves *minutemen,* because they claimed they could be ready to fight in sixty seconds.

The British had been hesitant to capture the rebel leaders, for fear that it would ignite a war. Now that the Americans were preparing for war anyway, the British decided that capturing Samuel Adams, John Hancock, and a few others might be the only way to cork the American volcano. Plans were begun to kidnap Adams and Hancock and ship them to England for trial

Patrick Henry of Virginia, the most famous speaker in American history

and execution, and there was even talk about murdering the two men. In the fall of 1774, unknown Loyalists circulated a letter among the redcoats in Boston advising them to kill fifteen men at the first sign of revolt. Samuel Adams headed the list, which also included John Hancock and Thomas Cushing. "Put the above persons to the sword, destroy their houses, and plunder their effects!" the letter advised.

In late 1774, rumors spread through the colonies that the British were bombarding Boston and that war had already begun. After one such false alarm, thousands of minutemen and other militiamen grabbed their muskets and set out for Boston to defend it from the enemy. Perhaps only one factor prevented war from breaking out in late 1774 or early 1775. In those days, armies generally avoided fighting in the wintertime, because cold weather could be deadlier than the enemy. Unaware of the plans being made for his capture, Samuel Adams used the winter inter-lude to write letters to his political friends around the country. He wanted to make certain that the thirteen colonies would do what their delegates to the First Continental Congress had pledged: help one another in case of war.

CHAPTER VIII

"Oh! What a Glorious Morning Is This!"

SAMUEL ADAMS SUSPECTED that the winter of 1774–75 would be the last peaceful season in America for some time. As he had anticipated, England rejected the Continental Congress's demands. With neither side budging, and with thousands of red-coats and Americans drilling in the Boston area, it did not require the Prophet Samuel to foresee that another incident like the Boston Massacre or Tea Party would spark a war.

The Massachusetts Provincial Congress met at Cambridge in early 1775 and voted to send the same four delegates, plus John Hancock, to the Second Continental Congress, scheduled to open in Philadelphia that May. The Provincial Congress also appointed a committee to spread the word that war seemed near. As its chairman, Samuel Adams wrote a resolution that was sent across Massachusetts:

> We have reason to apprehend that the sudden destruction of this Colony is intended, merely for refusing . . . tamely to submit to the most ignominious slavery. Therefore Resolved, That the great law of self-preservation calls

In this portrait of Samuel Adams based on the Copley painting, the artist gave him a gentler expression than usual.

upon the inhabitants of this Colony immediately to prepare against every attempt that may be made to attack them by surprise. . . .

The resolution went on to encourage the militia and minutemen to practice their marksmanship and "perfect themselves in military discipline."

Millions of schoolchildren have memorized the fact that the

American Revolution began on April 19, 1775, at Lexington, Massachusetts. It has gradually been forgotten that, if not for a broken egg, the war might have begun six weeks earlier in Boston. March 5 was a Sunday—a day reserved for religion in Boston—so the Massacre Day memorial was delayed twenty-four hours. Dr. Joseph Warren, one of the few Americans as eager for war as his friend Samuel Adams, was the scheduled speaker. Warren had answered the Loyalists' claim that Americans were cowards by saying, "I hope I shall die up to my knees in blood!" so the crowd that packed the Old South Meeting House on March 6 expected a very warlike speech.

Just before Dr. Warren's arrival, about forty fully armed British officers swaggered into the church. Perhaps one of the spies who

Most English people viewed Samuel Adams as a dangerous yet fascinating enemy. He is shown plotting war strategy against the British in this portrait created in England.

watched the enemy for Samuel Adams had informed him that the redcoats were coming, for he seemed to be the only person in the church unruffled by their arrival. A number of patriots in and near the Old South had weapons, too. Had the redcoats provoked a fight, Adams speculated in a letter to a friend a few days later, "not a man of them would have been spared." But a church was the last place Samuel Adams wanted the War for American Independence to begin, so he decided to treat the officers with extreme courtesy. As chairman of the event, he asked people sitting at the front of the church to move. He offered their seats to the redcoats, who also spilled onto the stairs of the speaker's pulpit.

Unknown to Adams, the soldiers intended to capture him, Hancock, and Warren inside the church. A soldier was to throw a raw egg at Dr. Warren while he spoke, as a signal for his fellow officers to seize the three men. However, upon entering the church, this soldier fell, dislocating his knee and splattering the egg. A London newspaper later claimed that only this accident prevented the British officers from attempting to arrest the three leaders.

The mood in the church grew tense as Warren spoke, for even though Samuel Adams told him to omit the most inflammatory parts, his oration still contained plenty to anger the redcoats. "We wildly stare about," said Dr. Warren, "and with amazement ask, 'Who has spread this ruin around us?'" He asked the audience if it was France, Spain, or the Indians. "No, none of these!" he answered. "It is the hand of Britain that inflicts the wound!"

The redcoats annoyed Dr. Warren and his audience by laughing and coughing to drown out his words. One officer sitting on the pulpit stairs held up a handful of bullets in front of Warren as a threat. The doctor tossed his handkerchief over the bullets and finished his speech. But when Samuel Adams stood up to propose that a speaker be appointed for the next year's commemoration, the redcoats shouted "Fie! Fie!" (an old word to express disgust).

Many in the audience mistook the shout for "Fire! Fire!" and were certain that the soldiers were about to start shooting. By chance, a regiment of redcoats passed the church just then, magnifying the crowd's fear that they were about to fall victim to another Boston Massacre. Many people had jumped out the church windows and were running down the street before they realized their mistake.

Samuel Adams traveled to Concord, twenty miles northwest of Boston, soon after Warren's speech. The Provincial Congress convened in Concord on March 22 and placed Adams in charge of a secret project. So intent was he on keeping the British in the dark about it that, rather than put anything in writing, he had messengers memorize his words. His couriers traveled to New Hampshire, Connecticut, and Rhode Island, where they spoke to leaders about organizing a New England army.

Whenever Samuel Adams was away from home, his spies kept him informed of what the British were doing in Boston. In mid-April, as the Provincial Congress was adjourning in Concord, Adams's spies sent him important information. It appeared that Governor Thomas Gage was going to attempt to arrest Samuel Adams and John Hancock at long last. The two patriots agreed that it was too dangerous for them to return to Boston. They decided to spend a few days in Lexington, between Boston and Concord, before heading to Philadelphia for the Second Continental Congress.

On April 15, Adams and Hancock traveled by carriage to Lexington, where they stayed at the home of John's cousins, the Reverend Jonas Clarke and his wife, Lucy. The eight-room house was already packed when the two men arrived. The Clarkes had ten children. Aunt Lydia Hancock and Dolly Quincy, who had become close friends, were also there, thanks to arrangements Hancock had made a few days earlier. With the house so crowded, Hancock's clerk John Lowell had to stay at nearby

Samuel Adams and John Hancock slept in this room in the Clarke house in Lexington.

Buckman Tavern with a huge trunk of papers belonging to the Massachusetts Provincial Congress.

Governor Gage had spies, too, and they informed him that Adams and Hancock were in Lexington, and that the patriots had stored a large quantity of military supplies at nearby Concord. As Adams and Hancock settled in at the Clarke home, Gage worked out details for what he hoped would be a double blow to the patriots. On the night of April 18, seven hundred soldiers would head out from Boston. They would capture Adams and Hancock in Lexington, then continue a short way west to seize the military supplies at Concord.

Patriots in Boston learned of Gage's plan. Some say a boy hired by British officers to watch their horses outside a tavern overheard them discussing the plot, while others claim that Gage's American wife informed the patriots of the scheme. The information was crucial, for it enabled Dr. Joseph Warren to send Paul Revere on the greatest mission of his life on the night of April 18, 1775. Revere was to warn Adams and Hancock in Lexington, and

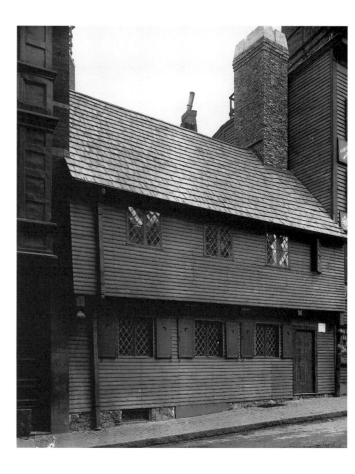

Paul Revere's house in Boston is still standing.

then the patriots in Concord, that the British were coming. Warren also sent William Dawes, another Son of Liberty, on a different route, so that the message could get through even if Revere were captured.

Before departing Boston, Revere stopped at the Old North Church. "Two lanterns!" he told a friend, who climbed up into the steeple and hung two lanterns in a window. This prearranged signal informed patriots near Boston that the redcoats were crossing the Charles River by ferryboat before marching inland. Had the British gone by land over Boston Neck, Revere would have ordered just one lantern hung in the church steeple. In his poem "Paul Revere's Ride," Henry Wadsworth Longfellow dramatized this incident by having Paul say, "One, if by land, and two, if by sea."

When he set out for Lexington at about 10 P.M., Revere was too busy evading redcoats to foresee that his every move that night would become part of American lore. Two friends rowed Revere across the Charles River to Charlestown (now part of Boston), where the forty-year-old silversmith borrowed a horse. Revere galloped up the road toward Lexington, warning people at farms along the way that the British were coming. Near Cambridge, two British officers almost seized him, but Paul veered away and continued up another road to Lexington.

Revere arrived at the Clarke house around midnight. He shouted and banged on the door so loudly that one of the eight Lexington militiamen guarding the home told him to stop making so much noise. "Noise!" Revere angrily replied. "You'll have noise enough before long! The Regulars [redcoats] are coming out!" The

The Old North Church, where two lanterns were hung on the night of April 18, 1775, at Paul Revere's order

commotion awoke Adams and Hancock, who were sharing a bedroom near the front door. When the two men saw Revere through the window, Hancock hurried to the door and told the guards, "Let him in!" Once inside, Paul warned the two leaders that the British were coming to arrest them. William Dawes soon arrived with the same news. Adams and Hancock sent one of the guards to ring the bell on the village green as a call for Lexington's militiamen to assemble. Then Samuel told John to gather his belongings and prepare to flee.

Hancock answered that he wasn't leaving Lexington. Instead, he would join the men on the village green and fight the redcoats.

Paul Revere's famous ride

When Samuel recovered from his shock, he realized that it was just like John to be so brave, unselfish, foolish, and childish all at the same time. As Lexington's bell summoned the townsmen to the green, Adams argued with Hancock in the Clarke kitchen. Samuel probably pointed out that they needn't worry about leaving the people in the Clarke house, for the British would not harm civilians. Perhaps he also mentioned that neither of them knew much about fighting. Samuel may have never fired a gun in his life, and although Hancock had commanded the Corps of Independent Cadets, it was mainly a ceremonial group that marched at important events in Boston. However, telling Hancock that he knew little about warfare wasn't the way to sway him, for it would only intensify his hotheaded bravery.

By one in the morning, about 130 Lexington militiamen, a third of them minutemen, had gathered on the green. Dolly Quincy later said that the men were a sorry sight, standing there in the damp grass in the middle of the night. Instead of uniforms, they wore everyday farm clothes. Instead of standard weapons, each carried whatever gun he owned. Fathers and sons stood shoulder to shoulder, and there were grandfathers among them, too. Although few people know it, the militiamen also included a black man. His name was Prince Estabrook, and he proved to be one of the best soldiers in Lexington.

Two hours passed, and still there was no sign of the redcoats. The British had taken longer than expected to leave the Boston area and were far behind schedule, but many of the men standing beneath the stars in the chilly air concluded that this was just another false alarm and that the enemy wasn't coming after all. Captain John Parker, their leader, finally allowed the men to leave, but warned that they must return immediately if the lookouts spotted the enemy approaching. Some men who lived near the green went home. Most went to Buckman Tavern, just across the green, to warm up over drinks.

After warning Hancock and Adams, Paul Revere and William Dawes continued toward Concord. On the way, they were joined by Dr. Samuel Prescott, who was returning home from sparking a female friend. Prescott's joining them was a stroke of luck, for he proved to be the only one of the three to reach Concord. Revere and Dawes were captured by a British patrol two miles short of Concord. A British major held a gun to Paul's head and threatened to blow out his brains if he did not answer his questions truthfully. Perhaps it was his experience as the father of sixteen children that enabled Paul to remain calm with a gun aimed at his head. He concocted a story that five hundred patriots were headed toward Lexington and boasted that he was responsible for assembling this army. Revere was released, but since he couldn't ride past the redcoats to Concord, he returned to Lexington to make sure Adams and Hancock were safe.

Revere reached the Clarke house around 3:30 A.M. and was astonished to find the two most important leaders in Massachusetts still arguing at the kitchen table. Revere listened impatiently as they talked on and on. Finally, Adams convinced Hancock that his country needed him more as a lawmaker than as a soldier. Years later, Dolly Quincy Hancock recalled that Samuel told John: "That [the fighting] is not our business. We belong to the Cabinet." This was said to be the first use of the word *cabinet* to describe important United States officials.

At about the time Hancock finally agreed to leave, a lookout galloped into town yelling, "The lobsterbacks are down the road!" Captain Parker ordered nineteen-year-old William Diamond to recall the men to the green by beating his drum. Hearing the call to arms, Hancock insisted on one more thing before he left Lexington. He went to the green and spoke briefly to the men, but what he said is not known. Once back at the Clarke house, Hancock arranged to meet Aunt Lydia and Dolly in a nearby

Kitchen where Samuel Adams and John Hancock argued

town. Then he, Adams, Revere, and John Lowell boarded a carriage. As the vehicle pulled away, Hancock sadly said, "If I had my musket, I would never turn my back on these troops."

While John Hancock sat brooding, Samuel Adams felt ecstatic. After writing thousands of letters and articles and organizing hundreds of political meetings over ten years, he was certain that the great moment was at hand. He and the three other men wanted to watch the encounter, so they stopped the carriage at a place in the woods outside Lexington from where they could see the village green. They had just entered their hiding place when Hancock remembered that the trunk containing the Provincial Congress papers had been left at Buckman Tavern. Revere and Lowell returned for the trunk while Hancock and Adams continued to watch from the woods.

At dawn, an advance party of several hundred redcoats under Major John Pitcairn arrived at Lexington. Captain John Parker watched them approach and realized that he had only about seventy troops on the green to fight them. The others had fallen asleep at home or had failed to return in time. "Stand your ground," Captain Parker reportedly told those seventy men and boys. "Don't fire unless fired upon. But if they mean to have a war, let it begin here!"

From Adams and Hancock's vantage point, the redcoats must have looked like toy soldiers as they approached and then halted about fifty yards from the patriots. Paul Revere and John Lowell were carrying the trunk from Buckman Tavern to a hiding place in the Clarke house as the British advanced. The two men knew it was foolish to stand there holding the trunk within shooting range of the redcoats, yet they continued to watch as though hypnotized. Perhaps they were close enough to hear Major Pitcairn's insulting words: "Disperse, ye rebels, ye villains, disperse, disperse in the name of the king! Lay down your arms!"

Major Pitcairn allowed Captain Parker to speak to his men for a minute. While the patriots discussed their situation, approximately forty bystanders of all ages looked on anxiously. They included Aunt Lydia Hancock, watching from the Clarke doorway, and Dolly Quincy, gazing out a bedchamber window. Revere and Lowell continued to watch, too, as did Adams and Hancock from their nook in the woods. Everyone knew that the next few seconds would determine whether America would be at war.

Despite the talk about standing their ground, Captain Parker and most of his men realized the truth now that British guns were pointed at them. They had no chance to defeat this larger, better-armed, and highly trained enemy. Captain Parker reluctantly told his men to keep their weapons but to go home without firing them. All but a few began to head home. Two who were ready to fight were Captain Parker's cousin, Jonas Parker, a grandfather who had vowed that he would never back down from a clash with the British, and Prince Estabrook, the lone black member of the Lexington militia.

Most of the Americans had taken a few steps toward home

when a shot was fired—from which side is not known to this day. Paul Revere and some other American witnesses insisted that a British officer on horseback fired his pistol. Major Pitcairn later claimed that an American behind a stone wall at the edge of Lexington Green fired his musket. In any case, the next instant the redcoats were shooting down the Americans, much as they had in the Boston Massacre five years earlier.

Jonas Parker was shot in the first British volley and fell to the ground, wounded. He continued to fire his musket while sitting on the ground until stopped forever by a British bayonet thrust. Isaac Muzzy also fell with a bullet wound and died right next to his horrified father. Jonathan Harrington, shot in the chest, crawled to his nearby house where he died in front of his wife and son. The Lexington men returned a few shots, but with little success. By the time the redcoats obeyed Major Pitcairn's repeated order to "Cease firing!" eight Americans lay dead. Ten patriots were wounded, including Prince Estabrook, who had been one of the few Americans to stand up to the British. The redcoats' only casualty was a man wounded in the leg.

From where he stood, Samuel Adams could not determine the outcome of the Battle of Lexington. But as he listened to the shooting and watched the clouds of gunsmoke rise above the miniature figures on the green, he knew that the Americans had fought the enemy. That was enough to make the dawn of April 19, 1775, the happiest moment of his life. As their carriage passed fields glistening in the rising sun, Adams told Hancock, in a burst of pure joy, "Oh! what a glorious morning is this!"

Adams and Hancock traveled several miles to the Widow Jones's house in Woburn. They sent a carriage for Aunt Lydia Hancock and Dolly Quincy, who told them about the battle and about a frightening close call. A bullet had just missed Aunt Lydia's head as she watched the fighting from the Clarkes'

The Battle of Lexington

doorway. The ladies and John Hancock were probably mystified that Samuel didn't seem much disturbed by the defeat. The important facts to him were that the American Revolution had begun and that the patriots might make a stronger stand at Concord.

Following their victory at Lexington, Major Pitcairn and his troops joined the rest of the British force and headed to Concord, five miles to the west. The redcoats approached Concord at about six-thirty in the morning. Thanks to Dr. Prescott's warning, the patriots in Concord knew of the British approach, and as word of the defeat at Lexington spread, men for miles around poured in to help defend the town. Still, the redcoats anticipated little trouble at Concord, for by this time they were convinced that the colonists lacked the nerve to fight them.

For several hours, this appeared to be the case. The Americans stood and watched forlornly as the redcoats confiscated gunpowder and weapons in the town. But when the British set the

Concord town hall and the liberty pole ablaze, something stirred in the Americans' hearts. At around ten in the morning, they advanced on approximately one hundred redcoats guarding Concord's North Bridge.

The redcoats fired warning shots into the water, but this time the patriots did not back off, nor did they retreat when the British fired their muskets directly at them, killing two men. "Fire, fellow soldiers, for God's sake, fire!" yelled an American officer. "Fire!" "Fire!" "Fire!" "Fire!" the Americans along the bridge shouted to one another. Suddenly hundreds of American bullets were flying at the British, killing three and wounding about ten of them.

For a few seconds the redcoats could not comprehend that the colonials had actually shot back. Then, realizing that they were outnumbered by an enemy that had found its courage, the British troops began a retreat to Boston. The Americans had an even greater shock in store for the fleeing enemy. Not satisfied with their victory at Concord's North Bridge, the patriots followed the redcoats, shooting at them from behind stone walls, trees, and barns.

As one redcoat after another was brought down, the remaining soldiers began to run in panic. Their deadly fire never ceasing, the Americans seemed to have fifteen thousand instead of fifteen hundred men. Near Lexington the British ran into some very angry acquaintances—Captain John Parker and those of his men who were still able to fight. A Lexington man had the pleasure of wounding Lieutenant Colonel Francis Smith, commander of the expedition.

A short time later, the redcoats passed rather close to the Widow Jones's home. Suddenly a Lexington patriot burst into the house yelling, "The British are coming!" Samuel Adams and John Hancock hid in a nearby swamp until there was no sign of the enemy, then fled a few miles through the woods to a house in

The Americans beat the redcoats at Concord's North Bridge . . .
. . . then chased the retreating redcoats back to Boston.

nearby Billerica. Late that night, Adams and Hancock learned the wonderful news. The Americans had chased the invaders almost to Boston, shooting at them all the way. If British reinforcements hadn't come out of Boston to help, all seven hundred soldiers on the Lexington and Concord expedition might have been killed. As it was, by the time the British entered Boston, nearly three hundred red-coats had been killed or wounded, as opposed to patriot losses of about a hundred.

Samuel Adams may have thought that it had proved to be a far more glorious day than even he had expected as he went to sleep on that spring night, for the colonists had shown that they could fight and beat large numbers of the enemy. Now his great hope was that his fellow congressmen in Philadelphia would cross the next barrier and declare independence from Great Britain.

List of the patriots killed and wounded in the Battles of Lexington and Concord. The names of several people we mentioned, including Jonas Parker and Prince Estabrook, can be seen.

CHAPTER IX

The Father of American Independence

*N*O ONE WAS MORE EAGER for the Second Continental Congress to open in the spring of 1775 than Samuel Adams. After spending several days in Worcester, Massachusetts, he and John Hancock set out for Philadelphia on April 27. Adoring crowds mobbed their carriage along the way, as the news spread that the British attempt to seize the two men had begun a war.

When they entered New York City or Philadelphia (reports disagree), something occurred that hinted at trouble ahead between Adams and Hancock. The crowd wanted to untie the horses and carry the coach with the two leaders inside it. Hancock was flattered by the offer of being borne through town like a king, but Adams disgustedly told him: "If you wish to be gratified in so humiliating a spectacle, I will get out and walk. I will not countenance an act by which my fellow-citizens degrade themselves into beasts." Although he agreed to keep the horses tied to the carriage, Hancock resented Adams for ruining his great moment.

The Second Continental Congress opened as scheduled on May 10, 1775, in the Pennsylvania State House. Samuel Adams had hoped that Congress would declare independence immediately, but, as was true of the general public, most of the delegates were still reluctant to take so drastic a step. Congress even decided to give England one more chance to make peace. Shortly after it opened, Congress sent the Olive Branch Petition to England asking that "harmony between [Britain] and these colonies may be restored." Samuel Adams was revolted by this paper, which received its name because the olive branch is a symbol of peace. Didn't his colleagues realize that the time for timid pleas had passed?

British officials tried to take advantage of the colonists' uncertainty by claiming that Samuel Adams and John Hancock were leading a good people to ruin. In June 1775, Massachusetts governor Thomas Gage issued this proclamation offering to pardon all but two of the American rebels:

> I do hereby in his Majesty's name offer and promise, his most gracious pardon to all persons who shall forthwith lay down their arms and return to the duties of peaceable subjects: excepting only from the benefit of such pardon SAMUEL ADAMS and JOHN HANCOCK, whose offenses are of too flagitious a nature to admit of any other considerations than that of condign punishment.

Flagitious means evil or villainous, and *condign punishment* implies a severe sentence, probably death by hanging. This offer of pardon didn't tempt the rebels any more than the Tea Act had. They might not be quite ready for independence, but they refused to let all the blame for the trouble between England and the colonies fall on the heads of Samuel Adams and John Hancock.

Around this time Adams began to compare the slow move toward independence to the birth of a child. "The child Independence is now struggling for birth," he wrote to a friend. "I trust that in a short time it will be brought forth, and . . . all America will hail the dignified stranger." Adams labored almost around the clock to assist in the birth. By day he worked on Continental Congress business. After eating supper at a waterfront tavern, he returned to his lodgings and wrote letters through the night to every corner of the thirteen colonies. "Declare independence immediately!" was his simple theme. What made his grueling schedule all the more remarkable was that his trembling had become worse with age, and on some days he found it difficult to write.

With his cousin's help, Samuel molded the Second Continental Congress into a more revolutionary body. Two weeks after the meeting convened, Peyton Randolph, president of Congress, had to leave Philadelphia and return to Virginia. Besides requiring a new president, the cousins realized, Congress had to organize an army and choose its commander.

Samuel and John Adams decided that these two major posts should go to men from Virginia and Massachusetts, which together contained nearly a third of the thirteen colonies' two and a half million people. The one choice would please the five southern colonies (Maryland, Virginia, North Carolina, South Carolina, and Georgia), while the other would satisfy the four New England colonies (Massachusetts, New Hampshire, Connecticut, and Rhode Island). The four middle colonies (New York, Pennsylvania, New Jersey, and Delaware) already had an important honor, for Philadelphia was hosting the Continental Congress.

The Adams cousins felt that John Hancock was the proper choice as president of Congress. Not only was Hancock a hero in New England, he was a man to whom the rich southern planters could relate. Thanks largely to Samuel and John Adams, Hancock was elected president of Congress on May 24, 1775. Several weeks later, the delegates were ready to create a national army and name its commander in chief. Before Congress was called to order on June 14, the cousins went for a walk in the Pennsylvania State House yard to hold a private conversation.

"No people that ever trod the stage of the world have had so glorious a prospect as now rises before the Americans," wrote Samuel Adams near the bottom of this article, published in the September 27, 1773, Boston Gazette *under the name "Observation."*

They decided that George Washington, a tall, quiet Virginian who wore his French and Indian War uniform to Congress, was the best man for the job.

That day Congress created the Continental Army (forerunner of the United States Army) and John Adams rose to nominate its commander in chief. President Hancock appeared pleased as John Adams began speaking, for he expected to win the post despite his lack of military experience. Two things happened when John Adams nominated George Washington. The tall Virginian rushed out of the chamber so the congressmen could talk about him freely, and Hancock looked crestfallen—an expression that intensified when Samuel Adams seconded the nomination. Besides wanting the post himself, Hancock remained hurt for years that the cousins hadn't informed him of their plan. In fairness to the Adamses, they never dreamed that Hancock, who already was president of Congress, also expected to command the army.

The cousins had more trouble persuading their colleagues to choose Washington than they had expected, for a number of them had other preferences. The cousins talked to their fellow delegates late into the night, using every argument they could think of. The next day, June 15, 1775, George Washington was elected commander in chief.

Congress ordered Washington to take command of the troops that had gathered to defend Boston from the British. But on June 17, 1775, before Washington could get there, a tremendous battle was fought in the hills of Charlestown. Known as the Battle of Bunker Hill, it was one of the deadliest clashes of the Revolution. The British proclaimed themselves the victors because they seized the hill they wanted, but the cost was high. More than a thousand redcoats were killed or wounded, compared to American losses of about four hundred. "A triumph indeed! We wish them twenty such victories!" Samuel Adams wrote to a friend, as he tried to keep up a brave front. Virtually everyone in the Boston area had lost a friend, relative, or neighbor in the fierce fighting. For the rest of his life, Adams grieved over the death at Bunker Hill of Joseph Warren, who had gotten his wish to "die up to my knees in blood." Besides serving as his son's medical teacher, the young doctor who had sent Paul Revere on his famous ride was probably the closest friend Samuel Adams ever had.

The Battle of Bunker Hill pushed the Americans closer to declaring independence, as did subsequent events. Not only did King George III reject the Olive Branch Petition, he began hiring thousands of German soldiers, called Hessians, to fight the colonists. By late 1775, about a third of all Americans were ready to declare the country independent, while another third remained loyal to England. The final third—patriots who were not quite ready for the giant step—were the group Samuel Adams hoped to sway with his letters and essays.

Ironically, a pamphlet written by an Englishman who had moved to Philadelphia gave the country the final nudge it needed. Thomas Paine's *Common Sense* was published in January 1776. The forty-seven-page pamphlet offered simple, sensible reasons why America should declare itself a new nation. For example, Paine argued that since an island couldn't possibly rule a continent forever, delaying independence would only leave the struggle to later generations. Few books in history have had as great an impact as *Common Sense*, which quickly sold an astonishing half-million copies. Ministers quoted from the pamphlet to their flocks, teachers read it aloud to their students, and people discussed it in taverns and on village greens.

Paine's arguments swung tens of thousands of undecided

Engraving of the British attack on Charlestown and the armies preparing to fight the Battle of Bunker Hill

The Battle of Bunker Hill convinced most people that there was no going back from war.

Americans into the independence camp. No one was more pleased than Samuel Adams, whom many people assumed was the author of the anonymously written pamphlet. In fact, Samuel Adams had done none of the writing, but Paine had borrowed some of his ideas, for the two men had become friends in Philadelphia.

Common Sense helped make 1776 the year of decision. The patriots in the colonies had formed their own legislatures, which began advising their congressional delegates to work for independence. North Carolina took the first step, instructing its delegates on April 12, 1776, to vote for separation from England. In May, Virginia told its delegates to propose independence. The honor of doing so went to Virginia's Richard Henry Lee, who on June 7, 1776, rose in Congress and read from a paper:

> Resolved, That these United Colonies are, and of right ought to be, free and independent States; that they are absolved from all allegiance to the British Crown; and that all political connection between them and the State of Great Britain is, and Ought to be, totally dissolved.

The honor of proposing independence went to Richard Henry Lee of Virginia.

The words *free and independent states* had a much more serious sound when proposed in Congress than when whispered in private, and many delegates wanted a few more weeks to consider the issue. Congress put off the vote on independence until early July 1776. But in case the vote came out for independence, Congress needed to have a paper ready explaining why the colonies were separating from Britain. Thomas Jefferson, whom Samuel Adams greatly admired, was asked to write this Declaration of Independence. The thirty-three-year-old redhead from Virginia sat down in his Philadelphia lodgings in late June

Thomas Jefferson (at far left) showing the Declaration of Independence to other members of Congress, including Benjamin Franklin (standing in the middle) and John Adams (standing at right)

George Washington watches on a white horse as the British leave Boston.

and went to work. After about two weeks, he had created a document that began "When in the Course of human events, it becomes necessary for one people to dissolve the political bands which have connected them with another . . ." and ended with the words ". . . we mutually pledge to each other our Lives, our Fortunes, and our sacred Honor."

The creation of the Declaration of Independence wasn't all that made the spring and early summer of 1776 a joyous time for Samuel Adams. On March 17—Saint Patrick's Day—George Washington and the Continental Army drove the redcoats out of Boston. However, not even this wonderful news could compare to the importance of the vote scheduled for early July.

Each of the thirteen colonies was to have a single vote on independence, based on the majority decision of its delegates at Congress. If a colony had seven delegates present, four had to vote for separation from England for that colony to choose independence. Samuel Adams knew that it would not be sufficient for eight or even ten colonies to choose independence. Unless the colonies were unanimous, they could end up fighting one another. In the days before the vote, Adams spoke privately with undecided delegates. Although none of these conversations was recorded, we have a letter Adams wrote on April 3, 1776, in which he presented his arguments to Dr. Samuel Cooper, a Boston minister. If we use this letter for our audio and exercise our imaginations for our video, we can eavesdrop on Adams as he deals with an undecided delegate over supper or while walking near the State House.

First, Adams listens intently as the man explains that he isn't ready to make up his mind. Once the fellow finishes, Samuel looks at him with his piercing eyes and asks in his quavering voice: "Is not America *already* independent? Why then not declare it?" Before the man can answer, Adams points a shaking finger at him and asks, "Can nations at war be said to be dependent either upon the other?"

"No," the man answers, willing to grant this point.

Adams smiles slightly, pleased at the delegate's fine sense. "I ask you again, why not declare for independence? Because, say some, it will forever shut the door of reconciliation. Upon what terms will Britain be reconciled with America? She will be reconciled upon our abjectly submitting to tyranny, and asking and receiving pardon for resisting it. Will this redound to the honor or safety of America?"

"No!" says the delegate.

"Surely, no!" echoes Adams, hoping that he has won another man over to the independence side.

On Monday, July 1, 1776—the day before the official vote—Congress debated the independence question. As the men argued, the sky outside grew so dark from an approaching storm that candles had to be lit in the chamber. Pennsylvania's John Dickinson, a leading opponent of independence and the author of the Olive Branch Petition, asserted that America was not yet ready to stand alone. John Adams took the floor to dispute the anti-independence men. Lightning flashed outside and thunder rattled the Pennsylvania State House as John gave one of the greatest speeches of his life. "For myself, I can only say this," declared John Adams. "All that I have, all that I am, all that I hope for in

Letter Samuel Adams wrote on April 3, 1776, in which he presented his "Is not America already independent?" argument

this life, I stake on our cause. For me the die is cast. Sink or swim, live or die, to survive or perish with my country, that is my unalterable resolution!" Thomas Jefferson related that the independence men stood and cheered John's speech.

Before ending their proceedings on that first day of July, Congress took a trial vote and found that nine colonies favored independence. The other four had major stumbling blocks. The majority of South Carolina's and Pennsylvania's delegates were not ready for separation from England. New York had told its delegates to abstain on the independence vote. Delaware had a special problem. Two of its delegates were split on the issue. The third, Caesar Rodney, favored independence, but he was in Delaware.

On July 1, a messenger sent from Philadelphia informed Rodney that he was desperately needed to swing Delaware's vote. Rodney set out that night in hope of riding nearly a hundred miles through stormy weather in less than twenty-four hours—a journey that even Paul Revere would have found difficult. While Caesar Rodney made his all-night ride, Samuel Adams worked furiously to make the vote unanimous. But when he finally went to sleep, he realized that it would take a miracle for all thirteen colonies to choose independence.

The delegates entered the State House on July 2, 1776, with a keen sense of anxiety. Before them lay a decision few people in world history had faced—whether or not to create a new nation. As New Hampshire delegate Josiah Bartlett wrote to a friend on the eve of the vote: "It is a Business of the greatest importance as the future happiness of America will Depend on it." Yet there was a light moment as Congress argued over the issue one last time. When a delegate insisted that America wasn't yet "ripe" for independence, New Jersey's John Witherspoon answered, "We are more than ripe for it! We are in danger of rotting for the lack of it!"

Late on July 2, the delegates realized that the hour had come to end the discussions and make the official vote. Everything fell into place better than Samuel Adams could have dreamed. The nine colonies that had favored independence the day before held firm. Two of Pennsylvania's anti-independence delegates decided not to vote, so that, as one of them said, their colony could obey "the voice of our country." This allowed Pennsylvania to squeak by for independence by a three-to-two vote. South Carolina changed its vote because it did not want to stand alone against the other colonies. And in a scene so dramatic it might not seem believable in a movie, a wet and exhausted Caesar Rodney reached Philadelphia in the nick of time to swing Delaware's vote for independence. (New York did not vote on July 2, but a few days later it made the decision unanimous.) With the July 2 vote, "the child Independence" was born at last and the thirteen colonies became the United States of America.

Samuel Adams and most other congressmen expected that the day of the vote for independence would be hailed as the nation's birthday. However, two days later, on July 4, 1776, Congress approved Thomas Jefferson's Declaration of Independence. That day John Hancock performed his most famous deed. As president of Congress, he became the first signer of the Declaration, which is why people who sign important papers to this day are said to be writing their "John Hancock." As he wrote his name in large, bold letters, Hancock reportedly said: "There! John Bull [a nickname for England] can read my name without spectacles and may double his reward on my head!" Later in the summer as Samuel Adams and other members of Congress signed the Declaration, Hancock warned the delegates that "There must be no pulling different ways. We must all hang together." Benjamin Franklin reportedly quipped, "Yes, we must indeed all hang together, or assuredly we shall all hang separately!"

Messengers carried copies of the Declaration of Independence

John Hancock signing his name on the Declaration of Independence on July 4, 1776

HE WROTE HIS NAME
WHERE ALL NATIONS
SHOULD BEHOLD IT
AND ALL TIME ⊂⊃
SHOULD NOT EFFACE
⊂⊃ IT ⊂⊃

to nearly every town in the newborn nation. It was read aloud from balconies of public buildings, on village greens, and everywhere else people met. In Philadelphia, the State House where the Declaration had been adopted became known as Independence Hall, and the bell in its tower that chimed the good news won fame as the Liberty Bell. In Boston, the Declaration was read from the balcony of the Old State House, and then "The bells rang . . . the cannon were discharged . . . and every face appeared

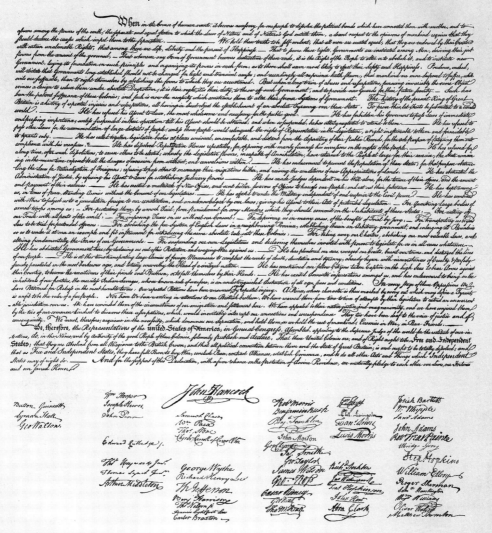

The Declaration of Independence. Samuel Adams's signature is at the far right, third from the top. He wrote "Saml" as a short form of Samuel but was not nicknamed Sam as many people mistakenly think.

The Declaration of Independence was read from the balcony of the Old State House in Boston.

joyful," Abigail Adams wrote to her husband John in Philadelphia.

Americans loved their Declaration of Independence as they have loved no public paper before or since. And because it said IN CONGRESS, JULY 4, 1776 at the top of the document, they began celebrating the Fourth of July as Independence Day. This practice has continued so long that few people today know that July 2 was really the nation's birthday.

The excitement began to fade as Americans realized that winning independence was far more difficult than declaring it. The United States was outclassed by England in every military category. In his New Year's Eve essay of 1773, Samuel Adams had boasted that "At the Beat of the Drum, she [America] can call five Hundred Thousand of her SONS to ARMS." His words were stirring, but untrue. George Washington's largest army during the war contained twenty thousand men, compared to fifty thousand for the British. Congress was so poor that it could not properly arm, feed, clothe, or pay its soldiers. At times many of the men fought barefoot and had to shoot squirrels and raid beehives to keep from starving. To make matters worse, most American soldiers signed up for short periods that ended, for example, on November 30 or December 31. This meant that George Washington had to schedule battles around certain dates!

Washington knew that his army was as yet too weak to win the war. For several years he tried to avoid losing the war by fighting small battles and making sneak attacks. Meanwhile, he trained his men, in the hope of one day fighting the huge battle he longed for as much as Samuel Adams had yearned for independence. As for the man who was becoming known as "the Father of American

The Liberty Bell in Philadelphia is one of the United States' most famous symbols. It was rung on July 8, 1776, to celebrate Congress's approval of the Declaration of Independence.

Independence," "the Chief of the Revolution," and "the Father of America," he spent the war years in Congress trying to provide George Washington with more soldiers and supplies. People even began to call Samuel Adams "the General" because of his efforts on behalf of the Army. But his greatest contribution during the war may have been his unshakable confidence that America would prevail.

By late 1777 the future seemed bleak for the patriots. That September the British invaded Pennsylvania, smashed the Americans at the Battle of Brandywine Creek, then marched toward Philadelphia. To prevent Benjamin Franklin's comment about them "all hanging together" from coming true, the delegates to Congress packed their papers and fled sixty-five miles west to Lancaster, Pennsylvania, which served as the national capital for one day—September 27, 1777. Seeking a safer haven, Congress

The Spirit of '76, *a famous painting created one hundred years later in 1876 by Archibald M. Willard, shows how the untrained American army contained young boys and old men.*

then moved twenty-five miles farther west to York, Pennsylvania, which was the U.S. capital from September 30, 1777, to June 27, 1778.

As was true among the public at this time, the morale in the U.S. government fell to an all-time low at York. Congressional attendance had generally been excellent in the exciting days of the Declaration of Independence, but there were days at York when the entire Congress consisted of Samuel Adams and about twenty other men, instead of the sixty-four delegates who were supposed to be there. At times, several states had no representatives present. Furthermore, some of the leading congressmen were gone or about to leave. When the government convened at York, Thomas Jefferson was back in Virginia serving as a lawmaker in his native state, and Benjamin Franklin was overseas trying to convince France to help America fight England. John Adams would soon sail for France to try to assist Franklin in his efforts, and John Hancock was about to leave Congress to spend a few months at home with Dolly Quincy Hancock, who had finally married him in the summer of 1775.

Most of the congressmen at York feared that Great Britain would soon turn the United States back into the thirteen colonies, much as Cinderella's coach turned back into a pumpkin at the stroke of midnight. Cornelius Harnett, who had recently arrived to represent North Carolina, expressed the gloomy mood in Congress in a letter he wrote on September 30, 1777, to Richard Caswell, the governor of his state. "I wish I had it in my power to give your Excellency a pleasing account of our affairs in this Quarter," Harnett wrote on the day Congress first met at York. The "Samuel Adams of North Carolina" then recounted the sad news of the British takeover of Philadelphia.

At this time of deep despair, one delegate seemed untroubled and certain of victory. Soon after Congress opened at York, a few delegates were discussing the hopelessness of the situation when

Adams surprised them with one of his rare speeches. It was so well planned that he must have prepared and saved it for just such a moment.

"Gentlemen," he began,

"Your spirits appear oppressed with the weight of the public calamities. Your sadness of countenance reveals your disquietude. A patriot may grieve at the distress of his country, but he will never despair of the common-wealth.

"Our affairs, it is said, are desperate! If this be our lan-guage, they are indeed. If we wear long faces, long faces will become fashionable. The eyes of the people are upon us. The tone of their feelings is regulated by ours. If we despond, public confidence is destroyed, the people will no longer yield their support to a hopeless contest, and American liberty is no more. But we are not driven to such narrow straits. Though fortune has been unpropi-tious, our condition is not desperate. Our burdens, though grievous, can be borne. Our losses, though great, can be retrieved. Through the darkness which shrouds our prospects, the ark of safety is visible. Despondency becomes not the dignity of our cause, nor the character of those who are its supporters.

"Let us awaken then, and evince a different spirit—a spirit that shall inspire the people with confidence in themselves and in us—a spirit that will encourage them to persevere in this glorious struggle, until their rights and liberties shall be established on a rock!

"We have proclaimed to the world our determination 'to die freemen, rather than to live as slaves.' We have appealed to Heaven for the justice of our cause, and in Heaven have we placed our trust. Numerous have been the manifestations of God's providence in sustaining us. In the gloomy period of adversity, we have had 'our cloud by day and pillar of fire by night.' We have been reduced to distress, and the arm of Omnipotence has raised us up. Let us still rely in humble confidence on Him who is mighty to save."

Samuel Adams then concluded his speech with a prediction. "Good tidings will soon arrive. We shall never be abandoned by Heaven while we act worthy of its aid and protection!"

Although moved by his words, his listeners may have thought Adams had lost his mind. Nearly everything was going wrong. Their army was so pathetic that Americans burst into tears when it marched by. The national government had been forced to make York, a town most Americans hadn't even heard of, the U.S. capital. Some states no longer seemed to care whether they were fully represented in Congress. Despite all this, the aging patriot with the quaking voice and shaking limbs was acting *cheerful*. The man who more than anyone else had led them into this situation was complaining about *their* defeatist attitude. The individual who would be the first to be executed if America lost the war was predicting that *"good tidings will soon arrive"*—without any apparent reason to think so!

What was the source of Samuel Adams's confidence? He felt certain that God would not let the United States be defeated and that there was a solid core of patriots who would never give up, even if it took a century to win independence. Several weeks later good tidings actually did arrive, probably convincing some of his fellow congressmen that Adams truly was the Prophet Samuel. On October 17, 1777, British general John Burgoyne was forced to surrender his five-thousand-man army after losing the Battle of Saratoga in New York State. This was the greatest American victory to that point, yet soon afterward the patriots again seemed on the brink of losing the war.

A few days before Christmas of 1777, George Washington led his eleven thousand men into winter quarters at Valley Forge,

Pennsylvania. As they marched into Valley Forge, the men left a trail of blood on the frozen ground, for half of them no longer had shoes. During that terrible winter more than three thousand American soldiers—over a quarter of the army—died of cold, hunger, and disease.

Then in the spring of 1778 came wonderful news from overseas. Thanks mostly to Benjamin Franklin's efforts, France decided to help the United States in its war against Britain. Suddenly the victory that nearly everyone except Samuel Adams had considered impossible seemed within reach.

The benefits of the alliance with France were felt almost immediately. The British fled Philadelphia in June 1778 because a huge French fleet was headed there. During the next three years the Americans and the French did well in land and sea battles.

Valley Forge. George Washington is the tall man wearing the cloak at left of center.

Finally, in 1781, came the chance George Washington had awaited since taking command more than six years earlier. That summer British general Charles Cornwallis, who had vowed to crush America "prostrate at my feet," led his eight thousand troops into Yorktown, Virginia. Washington followed Cornwallis to this small tobacco port with his army of seventeen thousand Americans and Frenchmen. Meanwhile, French ships blocked the escape route by sea.

The Americans and the French pounded the British day after day until the ground at Yorktown resembled the craters of the moon. By mid-October about six hundred British troops had been killed or wounded, and General Cornwallis realized that his situation was hopeless. On October 19, 1781, he surrendered his remaining troops to George Washington as a British band played a song called "The World Turned Upside Down." The Americans behaved with dignity at the surrender ceremony, but once the British marched away with their American guards, Washington's men began to jump about and sing. They knew that their country had won its independence, which Great Britain acknowledged when the peace treaty was signed in Paris, France, in September 1783.

Except for the Loyalists, Americans throughout the country rejoiced over the British surrender at Yorktown. Delirious with happiness and pride, adults drank thirteen toasts to the thirteen new states, politicians made long speeches, and crowds gathered to watch as towns fired thirteen-round cannon salutes. No one had more of a right to celebrate than the man who had worked longer than anyone else to make independence a reality. Yet just as he had been remarkably cheerful during the darkest days of the war, Samuel Adams was strangely subdued in victory. He had been certain of the outcome all along; now he was concerned about the kind of nation the United States would become.

CHAPTER X

The Prophet Samuel and the United States Constitution

$\mathcal{B}$Y 1780, Samuel Adams planned to retire from the Continental Congress. He was worn out from his eighty-hour work weeks, and he felt that the war would soon be won. Now fifty-eight years old, he was also eager to rejoin his family, whom he hadn't seen much since the troubles with England had begun.

As Adams wrapped up his affairs in Congress in late 1780, an event back home revealed a drop in his popularity. He was nominated for Secretary of Massachusetts, but lost the election to John Avery. Betsy Adams sent her husband a letter complaining about the voters' ingratitude, but on November 24 he wrote back saying that the people had the right to elect whomever they wanted:

> You seem, my Dear, to express more Concern than I think you ought, at certain Events [the election] that have of late taken Place in the Commonwealth of Massachusetts. Do you not consider that, in a free republic, the People have

an uncontrollable right of choosing whom they please, to take their Parts in the Administration of public Affairs? No man has a Claim on his Country, upon the Score of his having rendered public Service. It is the Duty of everyone to use his utmost Exertions in promoting the Cause of Liberty & Virtue; and having so done, if his Country thinks proper to call others to the arduous Task, he ought cheerfully . . . to console himself with the Contemplations of an honest Man in private Life. You know how ardently I have wished for the Sweets of Retirement. I am like to have my Wish. . . . If I live till the Spring, I will take my final Leave of Congress and return to Boston. . . .

He left the Continental Congress forever around April 19, 1781, the sixth anniversary of the Battle of Lexington. He made no farewell speech, and if any of his colleagues did so in his honor, it was against his wishes. Samuel Adams felt that lawmakers were fortunate to serve their country and should never be thanked with windy testimonials.

In late April, Adams reached home, which no longer meant the Purchase Street house. Around the time of the battles of Lexington and Concord, Samuel's family had gone to live with Betsy's father in Cambridge. British officers occupied the Adams home during their absence and wrecked it out of spite. So that the Adamses would have a roof over their heads in Boston, for a small fee the state legislature rented them the home of a British official who had fled the town.

His family was thrilled to have Samuel home to stay. Betsy had run the household without his help and companionship for six years, while Hannah, now twenty-five, had awaited her father's return to go ahead with an important event. Soon after Samuel reached Boston, Hannah married Thomas Wells, her stepmother's younger brother. Fortunately for family relations, Samuel liked

Thomas, who then became his son-in-law as well as his brother-in-law!

Hannah left home upon marrying, but twenty-nine-year-old Dr. Samuel Adams lived with his father and stepmother. His son's physical condition distressed Samuel Adams. During the war, the young doctor had served in the American army under such terrible conditions that his own health had collapsed. Suffering apparently from tuberculosis, he would never again practice medicine during his few remaining years.

Another member of the household has not been mentioned. Around the time of her marriage to Samuel, Betsy was given a young slave named Surry. Adams loathed the fact that all thirteen colonies allowed slavery and told Betsy: "A slave cannot live in my house. If she comes, she must be free." He filled out the papers to free Surry, who kept house for the family and lived with them for nearly fifty years. Surry was so devoted to Adams that she reportedly threatened to dump pots of hot food on the heads of people who argued politics with him. Surry must have done plenty of threatening after Samuel Adams's return, for he had entered an "out of fashion" period that would last nearly a decade.

In his absence, Adams's friends had nominated him not only for Secretary of Massachusetts, but also for the state senate. He won a senate seat and served for several years. Still, his admirers felt that he deserved something better. The governorship was out of the question, they realized. John Hancock, the most popular man in Massachusetts, easily won election as its first state governor in 1780, and, except for a two-year vacation, held the office for the rest of his life. Samuel Adams ran for lieutenant governor, his state's second-highest office, in 1783, but lost to his old friend Thomas Cushing. Several years later Fisher Ames, who was less than half Adams's age, defeated him for a seat in the U.S. Congress. Schoolchildren were already being taught that Samuel

Adams was the Father of the Revolution. Thomas Jefferson called him "the Man of the Revolution" and Pennsylvania lawmaker George Clymer said that "All good Americans should erect a statue to him in their hearts." Why, then, was Adams unable to win elections in his home state?

One reason was his ongoing quarrel with the idol of New England. Samuel Adams and John Hancock had argued before, but around 1777 they had a fight that left them bitter enemies. Both men seem to have been at fault. Adams had tried to keep his feelings about Hancock's expensive way of life to himself, but with American soldiers starving, he couldn't bear to see John living like a king and said so to other congressmen. Hancock found out, and a war of words ensued. Hancock had donated more money to the cause than Adams had earned in his life and deeply resented Samuel's criticism.

Things grew worse between them after that. In the late 1770s, a rumor that Adams was behind a plot to remove George Washington as army commander swept the nation. The truth was, Adams considered Washington overly cautious, but he was not part of the scheme to replace him. Still, the rumor damaged Adams's reputation, for after the war Washington was viewed as almost godlike, and anyone suspected of opposing him was considered unpatriotic. What stung Adams most was that Hancock, seeking revenge after their argument, apparently had started the rumor.

Younger Americans had their own reasons to be leery of Adams. When he lost the election for lieutenant governor in 1783, he was nearly sixty-one, which was old by eighteenth-century standards. The man who had once been the most rebellious person in America wasn't just old in years. His views seemed as outmoded as the Revolutionary-era clothing that he wore for the rest of his life. For example, he wanted to continue the tradition

This painting of George Washington rising to heaven as a godlike being was done shortly after his death in 1799.

of the Massacre Day speech, but in 1783 the younger generation ignored his protests and ended the yearly memorial. Younger people sought to repeal Boston's law banning plays and resented Adams's suggestions that their time would be better spent on working to improve the country than in the theater. Other Americans were ready to forgive the tens of thousands of Loyalists who had fled the United States, but Adams insisted that they were traitors who should never be allowed to return.

Samuel Adams also despised two postwar crazes. One was the fad for researching family trees to see if any British aristocrats were in the branches. He felt that people only wanted to learn about their ancestors so that they could act superior to their neighbors. When a friend offered to dig through his English ancestry, Samuel warned him not to because of the "scoundrels a further research might rake out." In addition, Adams opposed the military societies for Revolutionary War soldiers and their descendants that were formed after the war. He detested organizations that excluded people and feared that these soldiers' groups might grow into private armies.

Adams wasn't against *everything*, though, as some claimed. It was in his nature to fight for what he thought was just. Two of his favorite causes in his later years were the ending of slavery in the United States and the improvement of public schools so that children unable to afford private academies could have a good education. A favorite pastime of his old age was to visit schools to meet with the children and see what they were learning.

A pleasant change for Samuel Adams occurred in 1784. After renting the British official's home for a few years, the family moved into a house of its own next to a bakery on Winter Street. Family members later described the house as "dingy and weather-worn," but Samuel Adams seems to have found it comfortable because it reminded him of his old home on Purchase Street. He would live in the big, dilapidated house with faded yellow paint for the rest of his life.

When the young nation faced the first major crisis in its brief existence, it appeared that Adams would once again support the old way of doing things. Since 1781, the thirteen states had been held together by a weak set of agreements called the Articles of Confederation. Under the Articles, each state was in many ways stronger than the national government. The Continental Congress still had a president, but he had little power. The country had no national courts, and since the federal government lacked the authority to collect taxes, it could not pay all its bills. Moreover, there was no permanent U.S. capital, so Congress had to move from town to town like an unwanted orphan.

The central government was weak because most Americans

wanted it that way. The large and small states, the rich and poor states, the northern and southern states, each feared that the other would have too much control over a strong central government. Also, nearly everyone dreaded being taxed by a powerful U.S. government. The truth was, Americans felt much the same about taxation *with* representation as they had about taxation *without* representation.

Samuel Adams had been on the committee that created the Articles of Confederation, but that wasn't why he wanted to retain the document. Like most Americans during the nation's early years, he feared that a strong federal government would tax people and reduce the power of the states. He also wanted New England to remain as detached as possible from states he considered inferior. For example, New England had the nation's best schools, and, thanks partly to Adams's efforts, Massachusetts in 1780 had become the first state to outlaw slavery, while the south still relied on the evil practice.

Several events demonstrated that the national government needed more authority. In June 1783, about a hundred soldiers who were owed back pay by the U.S. government surrounded Philadelphia's Independence Hall, where Congress was meeting. They broke windows and shouted demands for their money. Lacking the funds, the congressmen packed their bags and moved the capital to Princeton, New Jersey. A few months later, when the capital was transferred to Annapolis, Maryland, the lawmakers faced another dilemma. The peace treaty ending the Revolutionary War wouldn't be official unless Congress signed and returned it to Paris, France, by March 3, 1784. At least nine states had to approve the treaty, but only seven were properly represented in Annapolis by late 1783. The treaty wasn't approved by Congress until Valentine's Day, 1784, and reached Paris a month late. Fortunately, England did not use America's tardiness to back out of the agreement. Shays' Rebellion, a revolt by farmers in western Massachusetts that took place in 1786–87, also illustrated the federal government's helplessness. The seven-hundred-man U.S. Army couldn't stop the rebellion, so the Massachusetts militia had to do the job.

By early 1787 there was a widespread feeling that the national government would collapse unless it were given more muscle. The question was: How much more? Many people, including Samuel Adams, wanted to strengthen the federal government somewhat by revising the Articles of Confederation. Another group preferred to create an entirely new set of national laws.

A convention to reorganize the federal government opened at Independence Hall in Philadelphia on May 25, 1787. Samuel Adams might have been selected as a Massachusetts delegate, but he did not want to attend a convention that he felt would create a very powerful central government. Virginia's Patrick Henry was among the other well-known lawmakers who decided not to attend for much the same reason.

When the convention began, the delegates themselves were unsure of what they would do. As it turned out, Samuel Adams and Patrick Henry were right—the convention hammered out a new framework of government, the U.S. Constitution. The delegates finished their work that September, then returned home to present the Constitution to their states. Immediately, Americans divided into two camps—Federalists who supported the Constitution and Anti-Federalists like Samuel Adams who opposed it. The two groups argued heatedly, for the Federalists were as convinced that the Constitution would save the nation as the Antis were that it would ruin the states.

Each state was to hold a convention at which it would ratify (approve) or reject the Constitution. If at least nine states ratified it, the Constitution would become the law of the land. But if fewer than nine approved, the Constitution would be scrapped and the Articles of Confederation would remain in effect. Delaware became known as the First State by approving the Constitution on December 7, 1787. Pennsylvania, New Jersey, Georgia, and Connecticut soon followed. The approval of just four more states was needed for the Constitution to take effect. But Americans began to realize that the Constitution needed the backing of all thirteen states to be effective, for how could there be national laws that weren't recognized by the whole country?

The Massachusetts convention to consider the Constitution opened in Boston on January 9, 1788. The eyes of the nation were on this meeting, for the Massachusetts decision would influence other states and could mean ultimate victory or defeat for the Constitution. It appears that slightly more than half the delegates were Antis when the convention opened. Looking back in time, we know that it was crucial for some of these opponents to change their minds, for, although not perfect, the Constitution has helped the nation survive world wars and other hard times. Had the United States remained under the Articles of Confederation, it might have been conquered by another country or possibly divided into several nations long ago.

Samuel Adams and John Hancock were elected as delegates to the Massachusetts Constitutional Convention, which proved to be one of the most difficult periods in both men's lives. The delegates had been debating for a few days when Dr. Samuel Adams's condition worsened. He died on January 17, 1788, with his father at his bedside. Samuel Adams opened the family Bible to the page where thirty-six years earlier he had written "Samuel Adams their second child was born Wednesday the 16 of October 1751, at one quarter of an hour after ten in the morning, and baptized the Sabbath following, by the Reverend Mr. Checkley." With a trembling hand he added the words: "and died January 17th,

1788." The convention recessed so that the delegates could attend the young doctor's funeral. Samuel Adams had always maintained his composure in public, and his faith in God had helped him endure many terrible losses, but at his only son's funeral he broke down and wept.

Something odd happened to Adams when the convention resumed. He had always been so firm in his opinions that there seemed to be a greater chance of Boston Harbor drying up than of his changing his mind. But now he gradually reversed his thinking about the Constitution. Exactly why is a mystery. Perhaps the Prophet Samuel gazed into the future once more and saw that the nation needed the Constitution, or perhaps he was swayed by the Federalists' arguments.

The final step of his transformation was accomplished in an unusual way. Everyone knew that Adams respected working people more than any other segment of the population. An informal meeting of workingmen was held at Boston's Green Dragon Tavern. These men, many of whom had been recruited by Adams for the Sons of Liberty more than twenty years earlier, passed resolutions supporting the Constitution. Paul Revere was sent to present these resolutions to Samuel Adams.

When Revere appeared at his door, Adams may have been reminded of the night that the silversmith warned him and Hancock of the redcoats' approach thirteen years earlier. Adams studied the resolutions and listened as Revere told him about the meeting. Then Samuel asked his old friend: "How many mechanics [workingmen] were at the Green Dragon when the resolutions were passed?"

"More, sir," answered Revere, "than the Green Dragon could hold."

"And where were the rest, Mr. Revere?" continued Adams.

"In the streets, sir," Revere explained.

As he aged, Samuel Adams was still known for his remarkable eyes.

"And how many were in the streets?"

"More, sir, than there are stars in the sky."

A similar visit seems to have won over Governor John Hancock. The governor did not attend the first few weeks of his state's constitutional debates, sending word that he was home sick with gout, a painful disease involving swelling of the joints. Since Hancock sometimes used his condition to avoid unpleasant situations, it was widely thought that he could have come to the convention had he wanted. His problem was that he craved to be on the popular side of every issue but couldn't yet tell how things stood at the convention. One day some pro-Constitution men appeared at Hancock's Beacon Hill mansion. They told him that it was in his power to save the nation, for Massachusetts would follow his lead, and New Hampshire and other states would follow Massachusetts. They may have also mentioned that Hancock might be elected to one of two important posts created by the Constitution—the presidency and vice presidency of the United States. Such flattery would have found its way into Hancock's heart and may have been what convinced him to support the Constitution.

Some of their friends had gotten Adams and Hancock at least to start speaking to each other a few months earlier. Now the two of them began plotting strategy concerning the Constitution at Hancock's home. They decided that they shared one reservation about the document. They wanted a bill of rights added that would guarantee certain basic rights such as freedom of speech and of religion.

John Hancock's friends carried him into the convention, where, on January 31, 1788, he rose from his chair, apologized for his feebleness, then gave a rousing pro-Constitution speech. Samuel Adams spoke in favor of the Constitution, too, and proposed a bill of rights. Together, Hancock and Adams convinced a number of wavering delegates to vote for the Constitution. Their efforts meant the difference between ratification and defeat, for when the votes were tallied on February 6, 1788, the totals stood at 187 in favor of the Constitution and 168 opposed. Had ten delegates voted against instead of for the Constitution, it would have lost by one vote.

The Massachusetts ratification set off a chain reaction. A few weeks later Maryland and South Carolina approved the Constitution, and then, on June 21, 1788, New Hampshire became the ninth state to register a yes vote. By the spring of 1790, all thirteen states had ratified it. Late the following year the Bill of Rights was added to the Constitution, with several articles similar to those Samuel Adams had proposed at the Massachusetts Constitutional Convention.

Adams and Hancock were now on speaking terms, but many of their friends felt that if they could cast aside all their old grudges toward each other, Massachusetts would benefit. By 1789, the two men had reached a point in life where they did not want to go to their graves hating anyone. They were both chronically ill—Adams with the trembling that often prevented him from writing and Hancock with the gout that often left him unable to walk. Both had also suffered the deaths of children—Adams his only son and John and Dolly Hancock both their children when very young. In the spring of 1789 the two patriots took the last difficult steps and forgave each other for past wrongs, real or imagined. They celebrated by running on the same ticket, Hancock for governor, and Adams for lieutenant governor. They won easily and wore identical American-made suits at their inauguration to show a spirit of togetherness.

The Massachusetts lieutenant governor had little responsibility except to advise the governor when asked and to be ready to step into the job should the governor die. Since Adams was more than fourteen years older than Governor Hancock, everyone expected him to serve as lieutenant governor for a time, then retire to his books and garden.

In the summer of 1793, John Hancock's health worsened dramatically. He would not leave his house and did not want people to see him. Samuel Adams had to communicate with Hancock through letters. On September 3, Adams sent Hancock a get-well note in which he mentioned that he would always treasure a certain letter of John's. Two weeks later, Hancock summoned the strength to attend the Massachusetts legislature one last time, but when he arrived he could not stand up or say what he intended. On October 8, a message was sent to Samuel Adams. John Hancock, his companion on the most "glorious morning" of his life eighteen years earlier, had died that morning. Amid all the memories of his stormy relationship with Hancock, Adams also realized that, at the age of seventy-one, he was now the governor of Massachusetts.

CHAPTER XI

"We Are Now in Port"

JOHN HANCOCK WAS as impressive in death as he had been in life. His funeral procession was the largest ever held in New England up to that time. Twenty thousand people marched in it— equivalent to Boston's entire population. Samuel Adams, the new governor, led the mourners. Also near the head of the procession was John Adams, who since 1789 had been serving under President George Washington as the nation's first vice president.

The route took Samuel Adams past many places filled with memories. As the mourners left the Hancock mansion, perhaps Samuel recalled how twenty-seven years earlier he had glanced toward Beacon Hill and asked, "Is there not another John that may do better?" While crossing Boston Common, he may have remembered telling his cousin after the 1766 election: "This town has done a wise thing today." A short way from the Common, the mourners came to the site of the Liberty Tree, where Samuel Adams had orchestrated protests against the Stamp and Tea Acts. The British had cut down the tree in 1775 during their occupation of Boston, but Samuel Adams stopped the procession at the memorial known as the Liberty Pole that had been placed

John Adams in his later years

on the spot. As he led the long line of people around the Old State House, the new governor may have thought back to the day after the Boston Massacre, when he demanded of Governor Hutchinson: "Both regiments or none!" But near the Boston Massacre site, Samuel Adams could no longer continue. Emotion and fatigue had so weakened him that he had to return home before the mourners reached the Granary Burial Ground.

Samuel Adams had hoped to retire after serving for a few years as lieutenant governor. He had grandchildren now—Hannah and her husband had a daughter and two sons—and he wanted to spend time with them. The large salary that came with the governorship didn't have any appeal for him, either, because he was at long last financially secure. In the early 1790s, the U.S. government paid Samuel about $5,000 that it had owed his son for his wartime service, which meant that, in his seventies, Adams could finally survive without his friends' help. He used some of the inheritance to pay for the Winter Street home.

The new governor looked as decrepit as his old yellow house next to the bakery. His head trembled quite a bit when he spoke, and he had such difficulty holding a pen that other people had to write his state papers as he dictated. Those who did this for him included his oldest grandchild, Elizabeth, who was ten years old when he took office. Yet, in many ways, holding the highest office in Massachusetts was a fountain of youth for Samuel Adams, who to this day holds the record as the oldest governor the state has had. Not only did he resume his long workdays and recapture his enthusiasm of revolutionary times, he seemed to be pleasanter than ever before. He was more tolerant of other people's views, and he showed a willingness to change his mind that astounded his old friends. Governor Adams also had good relations with the legislature, partly because he didn't like to veto (kill) bills it passed. When asked why he disdained his veto power, he said that one person could never be as wise as a large group of lawmakers.

The election for Massachusetts governor was held yearly in Samuel Adams's time. After completing the few remaining months of Hancock's term, Adams ran for governor on his own in the spring of 1794. His opponents called him too old to be governor, but on Election Day the voters made him their overwhelming choice, as they did again in 1795 and 1796.

The working people, who still viewed him as their champion, were the governor's strongest supporters. Adams retained his habit from childhood of walking about the waterfront taverns to learn what the people were thinking, and he also traveled about

Boston on foot on government business. Some people complained that their chief executive should ride in style, as Governor Hancock had done, so shortly after Adams's victory in 1794, he was visited by a group of prominent men who presented him with a beautiful new carriage and a pair of horses. Adams was opposed to public officials accepting gifts, but since he didn't want to insult his visitors, he accepted the carriage and horses as a loan. Nevertheless, he continued to walk to most of his appointments, which prompted a young lawyer to lecture him about destroying the dignity of the governorship. Samuel Adams responded: "The Almighty gave me two feet for the purpose of using them, sir! I have been walking through the streets of Boston for seven decades, and shall continue to do so until I can no longer walk!"

Governor Samuel Adams

A highlight of Adams's three and a half years as governor occurred on July 4, 1795. On that nineteenth anniversary of the adoption of the Declaration of Independence, Paul Revere helped him lay the cornerstone of a new State House. Two centuries later, this building remains the capitol building of the Bay State. The only major crisis Adams faced as governor also took place in 1795. Early that year news arrived that the Jay Treaty between the United States and Britain had been signed in London in November 1794. Many Americans including Samuel Adams opposed the treaty, for it failed to prevent U.S. sailors from being forced to serve in the British Navy. Bostonians protested the Jay Treaty by breaking windows, burning a British ship in Boston Harbor, and parading about town with watermelons cut into the shape of ugly faces. About two hundred people petitioned Governor Adams to call out the militia against the rioters, but he refused, saying it had been "only a watermelon frolic." Who knew better than Samuel Adams what could happen when soldiers were called out against the Bostonians?

Samuel Adams's popularity may have been at an all-time high by 1796. So many Americans approved his views on the Jay Treaty and admired how he governed his state that there was a movement to elect him president that year. Had he been twenty years younger, he might have sought and won the nation's highest office. As it was, he received a handful of electoral votes even though he did not want the presidency, which was won by his cousin John Adams.

In January 1797, seventy-four-year-old Samuel Adams made a speech to the legislature in which he announced that he would not seek reelection that spring. "The infirmities of age render me an unfit person in my own opinion," he said, "and very probably in the opinion of others, to continue in my station." People who were "too warmly attached" to him should not waste their votes on him, he insisted, for he would not serve if reelected. Adams concluded his speech by saying: "When I shall be released from the burdens of my public station, I shall not forget my country. Her welfare and happiness, her peace and prosperity, her liberty and independence, will always have a great share in the best wishes of my heart." His reference to "liberty and independence" in the last sentence of his farewell speech was fitting, for perhaps no person who ever lived used these words as often as Adams did.

Increase Sumner was elected governor to succeed Samuel Adams in May 1797. The ex-governor returned the carriage and horses and retired to his Winter Street home. After serving his town, colony, state, and country for nearly half a century, he looked forward to a time of rest.

His last years were as peaceful and happy as he could have hoped. Hannah and her three children spent a great deal of time at the old yellow house. His granddaughter, Elizabeth, continued to write his letters for him. And since he could no longer see well, even with his glasses, Elizabeth and her two brothers took turns reading the Boston newspapers to him.

Old friends who came to visit noticed a change in Samuel Adams. Previously, he had always been too busy to reminisce about the past. Now he did not want to talk about much except revolutionary days. When the conversation turned to other subjects, he brought it back to the Stamp Act, the Tea Party, and the spring morning when he and John Hancock watched an

OPPOSITE: *His granddaughter, Elizabeth, or someone else wrote this letter for Samuel Adams dated December 10, 1800, but he signed it himself. His signature is very shaky compared to the one on the Declaration of Independence (on page 131) of twenty-four years earlier. Addressed to Pennsylvania governor Thomas McKean, this letter was intended to help a young descendant of Boston's founder, John Winthrop.*

Boston Dec.r 10th 1800.

I am very happy, with your leave, to introduce
the young Gentleman who is the bearer of this letter.
It is his own request. He descended from that
illustrious man Govenor John Winthrop, th leader
of our first & renowned ancestors; leaving, what
was called in those days a handsome fortune, that
he might plant the seeds of religion knowledge
& liberty in this, as they termed it, outside of the
world. His descendants have hitherto sustained
his principles & manners. The grandfather of this
youth was John Winthrop Esq.r —the learned
professor— of mathematicks & naural
philosophy — at Harvard College & fellow of the
royal sosiety in England ————————The youth
I now recommend, though but 22 years of age
has been a considerable traveler in Europe.
If you can spare any portion of your time
to countenance & instruct him, you will very
much gratify ——

Your sincere friend & affectionate
fellow citizen
Saml Adams

Thomas McKean Govenor of
Pensylvania

untrained group of men and boys begin the war for independence.

Samuel was no longer close to his cousin in his last years. After spending nearly a decade on government business in Europe, John Adams had come home convinced that the people did not always know what was best and the rule of kings and queens had much to recommend it. He brought some of these aristocratic views to his term as president. For example, President John Adams agreed to the Alien and Sedition Acts of 1798, which subjected people, especially foreigners, to jail and other severe penalties for criticizing the U.S. government. Were he ten years younger, Samuel probably would have been the leading foe of the Alien and Sedition Acts and might have challenged his cousin to send him to jail. But many other people took up the fight, and the laws were phased out.

Samuel Adams had more respect for the next president, Thomas Jefferson. Shortly after he was elected in 1801, Jefferson wrote Adams a letter in which he admitted that, while preparing his inaugural address to the nation, he wondered what his "dear and ancient friend" Samuel Adams would think of the speech. "In meditating the matter of that address," he explained, "I often asked myself, Is this exactly in the spirit of the patriarch Samuel Adams? Will he approve of it? I have felt a great deal for our country in the times we have seen, but individually for no one so much as yourself."

In his reply, Samuel Adams expressed his faith that the nation had weathered its most difficult times. "The storm is over and we are now in port," Samuel assured his old friend. He offered his prayer that, under President Jefferson, "May Heaven grant that the principles of liberty and virtue, truth and justice, pervade the whole earth." He also offered a humorous explanation about why he was resisting the temptation to give Jefferson advice:

An old man is apt to flatter himself that he . . . can instruct [the young] by his experience, when in all probability he has forgotten every trace of it that was worth his memory. Be assured that my esteem for you is as cordial, if possible, as yours is to me. Though an old man cannot advise you, he can give you his blessing. You have my blessing and my prayers.

SAMUEL ADAMS

Adams celebrated his eightieth birthday in 1802. Although too feeble to go far from home, he sometimes walked a few steps in front of his house or strolled through his garden in his nightgown and cap. By the fall of 1803, even this was too difficult for him, and he began spending much of the day in bed. His mind often wandered, but he was still lucid enough to make a final request. Sometime around his eighty-first birthday on September 27, 1803, he gathered his loved ones and told them that he despised the idea of an elaborate funeral and that they should bury him in the plainest coffin.

Near dawn of October 2, 1803, Samuel Adams had difficulty breathing. His doctor, Charles Jarvis, told the family that his final moment was near. A few minutes past seven on that Sunday morning, Samuel Adams whispered a few words. As Betsy Adams bent over her husband to hear what he was saying, he took his last breath, eighty-one years and five days after he had been born on another Sunday morning.

News of Samuel Adams's death quickly spread through the nation he had done so much to create. Newspapers ran stories praising the great patriot, including this article in the Boston *Independent Chronicle*:

SAMUEL ADAMS IS DEAD!

We have the painful task to announce to the public, that on yesterday morning, about a quarter past seven o'clock,

The Father of American Independence as he looked near the end of his life

S.Harris.sc.

at his house in this town, died in the eighty-second year of his age, SAMUEL ADAMS . . . a prodigy of talents and industry of which the lapse of ages will not produce a parallel.

In his useful career, he seemed occupied with but one sentiment; and that comprehended every circumstance which had any relation to the interests and independence of his native country, and the rights and liberty of the human race.

The foe of tyrants in every form, the friend of virtue and *her* friends, he died beloved, as he had lived

respected. Admiring posterity . . . will emphatically hail
him as the undeviating friend of civil and religious liberty,
and the FATHER OF THE AMERICAN REVOLUTION! . . .

The funeral, we understand, will be from his late
dwelling-house in Winter Street on Thursday next, at four
o'clock, P.M. The friends of our POLITICAL PARENT, in
this and the neighboring towns, are requested to attend.

His family and friends discussed the kind of funeral Samuel
Adams should have. Since he had loved young people, some
favored a procession of schoolchildren. Others argued for a procession of the survivors of the Battle of Lexington, since the start
of the Revolution had been his favorite moment in life. Adams
would have liked both ideas, but since agreement could not be
reached, the very thing that he hated occurred: His funeral turned
into "the usual parade," as his friend Judge James Sullivan commented.

The day of the funeral, Boston shops closed, bells tolled, ships
flew their flags at half-mast, and cannons were fired. A large procession including many U.S. and Massachusetts officials accompanied Adams's family to the Granary Burial Ground. In Washington, D.C., which had become the nation's permanent capital in
1800, members of the U.S. Senate and House of Representatives
wore mourning bands on their arms for a few weeks following
Adams's death. His plain coffin was the only part of Samuel
Adams's last request that was honored. However, many people
were appalled that so great a man was buried in a coffin more
appropriate for a pauper. Fifty-four years later, in 1857, Samuel
Adams's body was unearthed, placed in a fancy coffin with the
letters *S.A.* on it, and reburied.

The Americans of 1803 knew that they had lost one of the most
important of the Founding Fathers. Just eight days after Samuel
Adams's death, Judge James Sullivan published an article about

him in the *Independent Chronicle* in which he exclaimed: "To give his history at full length would be to give a history of the American Revolution." Sullivan and everyone else who knew about his accomplishments expected that Samuel Adams would be remembered forever as the Father of the Revolution and the Father of American Independence. The Father of Human Independence might be an even more fitting nickname, for the American Revolution has inspired dozens of other successful fights against colonial rule in Mexico, Canada, and many countries in Africa, Asia, Central and South America, and other lands. Billions of people who are alive today owe their freedom—at least in some measure—to the man who began the struggle for American independence.

But as time passed, his home country forgot that Samuel Adams had been the firebrand of independence. Later generations have given the bulk of the credit for the founding of the United States to George Washington, John Hancock, Thomas Jefferson, and John Adams. If they know of Samuel Adams at all, most people today associate him with the Boston Tea Party, without being certain of his connection. Samuel Adams would be the last person to complain about being neglected, though, for he always tried to stay in the background while others received the praise. Besides, he had helped create the only memorial he ever wanted, a living and growing legacy that has flourished for two hundred years since his death—the United States of America.

In the Footsteps of Samuel Adams

THE UNITED STATES has thousands of reminders of its Founding Fathers. Across the land there are towns, counties, parks, and streets named Washington, Adams (nearly always for John Adams), Jefferson, and Hancock. In addition, some of the Founding Fathers' homes have been preserved. Mount Vernon, George Washington's Virginia home, has our first president's false teeth, his Revolutionary War trunk, and the bed in which he died. Also in Virginia is Monticello, Thomas Jefferson's home, where visitors can see a large clock Jefferson designed that tells the days of the week. The birthplace of our second president, John Adams, is a famous landmark in what is now Quincy, Massachusetts, and in downtown Boston stands Paul Revere's house, where visitors view silver objects made by Paul and marvel how the Reveres raised sixteen children in such small quarters.

What about Samuel Adams? In northwest Massachusetts is the town of Adams, the birthplace of women's rights leader Susan B. Anthony. Adams and nearby North Adams may be the only two

Adamses in the nation that were named for Samuel, not John. There is also a statue of Samuel Adams in the U.S. Capitol in Washington, D.C. In 1864, Congress invited each state to send statues of two of its most prominent people to be displayed in the Capitol. On the nation's one hundredth birthday in 1876, the Bay State sent statues of John Winthrop, the founder of Boston, and Samuel Adams. Created by Anne Whitney, the Samuel Adams statue can be seen in the Capitol's East Central Hall. Today many people are puzzled by the choice of Samuel Adams over John and John Quincy Adams, the only father and son who both served as president. But in 1876, Samuel Adams was considered to be without question the greatest person ever born in Massachusetts.

Writer George Sand called Samuel Adams "the most persuasive political writer in all history." Certainly no other American before or since has written as many letters to newspapers and political leaders. Where are all his letters? In the eighteenth century, people usually made at least two copies of a letter—one to send and one to retain for their records. We have hundreds of Adams's letters, but thousands of others were destroyed.

One day when the Adams cousins were at the Continental Congress, John visited Samuel in his room. In John's own words, he watched as his cousin "cut up with his scissors whole bundles of letters in atoms that could never be reunited, and threw them out the window to be scattered by the winds." This disturbed John, who preserved copies of his letters and recorded the details of his daily life in his diary for the benefit of posterity. When John asked how he could destroy such historic documents, Samuel answered, "Whatever becomes of me, my friends shall never suffer by my negligence," meaning that he didn't want his friends embarrassed by the contents of the letters.

Even after he destroyed these letters, many more bundles remained. His family found trunks and boxes of letters and other papers in the attic following Samuel Adams's death in 1803. They let autograph hunters take some as mementos, but many of the other papers met an unusual end. A family servant, perhaps Surry, used piles of Samuel Adams's letters to kindle the fireplace. The Grand Incendiary might chuckle to know that letters he wrote to spark the Revolution went up the chimney in ashes.

I obtained photos of surviving Samuel Adams letters for this book, but the libraries and museums that own the original documents do not let people handle them. This left me with a craving to locate something personal of Samuel's. Perhaps his Purchase Street birthplace or his Winter Street home was still standing. Perhaps tucked away in a museum attic was his old red cloak or the wardrobe with the liberty cap emblems his friends gave him to wear at the Continental Congress. Perhaps somewhere in Boston lived Samuel's great-great-great-great-granddaughter, who would let me examine the Bible in which he recorded the family history.

I began my search by contacting the Boston Beer Company, makers of Samuel Adams Boston Lager, each bottle of which bears a portrait of the patriot on the label. Since Samuel was a brewer, I hoped that the beer named for him was made by his descendants. However, it turned out that, despite using the name Samuel Adams, the firm is not a continuation of his brewery, and no descendants of his are involved in the operation.

The search continued through phone calls and letters. I contacted the National Archives, the Library of Congress, and the Smithsonian Institution, all in Washington, D.C. In Boston, I questioned numerous libraries and museums ranging from the Massachusetts State Archives to the Boston Tea Party Museum, and elsewhere in the state I spoke to such places as Minuteman National Park and the American Antiquarian Society. None had so much as a button that had belonged to Adams, nor did they know

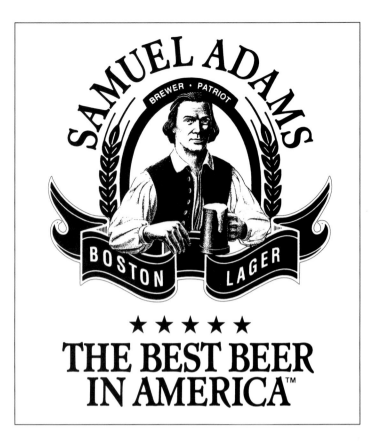

Picture of Samuel Adams on the label of Samuel Adams Boston Lager

of any living descendants of his. As for his houses, both were taken down long ago. The closest I came to pay dirt was at the Bostonian Society, which has two mugs that Samuel *may* have drunk from, but this hardly quenched my thirst for contact with my hero.

Since touching something that had belonged to Samuel Adams seemed impossible, I decided to do the next-best thing. I would visit sites connected with Adams in the Boston area, make a pilgrimage to his burial place, and track down the spots where his homes once stood to see what is there today. I booked a flight to Boston for mid-April, for, while following in Samuel's footsteps, I also wanted to see the reenactment of the first battle of the Revolution, held around April 19 at Lexington.

Downtown Boston today is a mixture of modern skyscrapers and historic old buildings. Fortified with maps, I located Samuel's birthsite not far from Boston Common, the big park that is a haven from the speeding traffic on nearby thoroughfares. The man who was incapable of handling money might laugh to know that an office tower, housing investment and life insurance firms, stands on the site of his Purchase Street home. No plaque describes the location as the birthplace of Samuel Adams.

Next I looked for 10 Winter Street, where he lived his last years. The narrow cobblestone street, lined with shops, retains an old-fashioned flavor, complete with a policeman on horseback. The April morning was cold, so while searching for number ten, I stopped at a stand for a cup of hot tea. Shortly afterward, I located the spot, occupied by a clothing store for overweight people. On a side wall facing the alley, there is a small plaque, green with age, that perhaps a few people have noticed:

ON THIS SITE ONCE STOOD THE HOME OF SAMUEL ADAMS WHO BOUGHT IT IN MAY 1784 AND DIED IN IT OCTOBER 2, 1802. IN GRATEFUL MEMORY OF THE FATHER OF THE REVOLUTION THIS TABLET IS PLACED BY THE MASSACHUSETTS SOCIETY OF SONS OF THE REVOLUTION   1893

The plaque recorded his death a year too soon, yet seeing that Adams was still known as the Father of the Revolution a century before my visit warmed me more than the tea did. Somehow, though, the drink in my hand seemed an insult to the planner of the Boston Tea Party, so I dumped it in a garbage bin before heading on to Faneuil Hall and the Old South Meeting House.

There was more good news at Faneuil, which looks much as it did when Adams spoke there to the townspeople. Outside the hall is a twenty-foot-tall statue of the patriot inscribed with the words:

SAMUEL ADAMS 1722–1803
A PATRIOT, HE ORGANIZED THE REVOLUTION
AND SIGNED THE DECLARATION OF INDEPENDENCE.
GOVERNOR, TRUE LEADER OF THE PEOPLE,
A STATESMAN INCORRUPTIBLE AND FEARLESS

A ranger inside the hall showed me where Samuel Adams had stood and spoken to the town meetings. Then he made an interesting comment: "Unlike the other revolutionaries, Samuel Adams is controversial even today. People still don't know what to make of him." Even historians disagree about Adams, he explained. Some see him as an indomitable fighter for liberty, while others view him as a conniver who distorted the truth to get his way. Of course, he was really both.

Nearby, at the Old South Meeting House, a group of schoolchildren were sitting in the pews. They had scripts and were acting out the town meeting before the Boston Tea Party. "Who knows how tea will mingle with salt water?" shouted a student defiantly. Then a miniature Samuel Adams arose and said, "This meeting can do nothing more to save the country!"

Amazingly, some of the tea from the Boston Tea Party has been preserved. The Old State House, where Adams presided as Massachusetts governor, has a bottleful of it, as does the Old North Church, where Paul Revere arranged for lanterns to signal the British approach toward Lexington in April 1775. The story of how the tea was preserved is the same at both places. An "Indian" at the Tea Party later found that some tea had fallen into his boots and saved it for posterity.

One place that I visited I expected to be sad, but the moment I entered the Granary Burial Ground, I felt among friends. Samuel Adams is certainly among friends there. His grave, which is located beneath a linden tree at the front of the cemetery, is marked by a plain stone that says:

HERE LIES BURIED SAMUEL ADAMS
SIGNER OF THE DECLARATION OF INDEPENDENCE
GOVERNOR OF THIS COMMONWEALTH
A LEADER OF MEN AND AN ARDENT PATRIOT
BORN 1722   DIED 1803

Next to him are buried Christopher Snider, the twelve-year-old shot by the Loyalist Ebenezer Richardson, as well as Samuel Gray, Samuel Maverick, James Caldwell, Crispus Attucks, and Patrick Carr, all victims of the brawl Samuel Adams named the Boston Massacre. Farther back in the little cemetery, beneath a monument four times the height of Adams's, is John Hancock's grave. Paul Revere also lies in the Granary Burial Ground, as does James Otis, who inflamed Boston with his cry of "Taxation without representation is tyranny!"

Leaving Samuel in good company, I continued on to Lexington for the reenactment of the war's first battle. In 1775, the redcoats took several hours to reach Lexington; now the trip from Boston can be made by automobile in minutes. Lexington was swarming with visitors when I arrived, for Massachusetts celebrates the anniversary of the Battle of Lexington as Patriots' Day. Schools and some businesses close, and people from across New England and beyond visit Lexington to see the men of the town act out the famous battle.

The afternoon before the reenactment, I visited the Reverend Jonas Clarke house. It looks much as it did the night of April 18–19, 1775, when Adams and Hancock were awakened by Revere's shouts that "The Regulars are coming out!" Several items relating to the battle are preserved in glass cases at the house. The drum young William Diamond beat to summon the men to the green can be seen, as can British major John Pitcairn's pistols. When I spotted an old vest, for an instant my hopes rose that it was Samuel's, but it proved to be John Hancock's. Still, visitors can see the bedroom where Adams and Hancock were sleeping when Revere awakened them, and the kitchen has the big table where Adams talked Hancock out of fighting in the battle.

The excitement in Lexington grew on the evening of the eighteenth. Throughout town, people could be heard discussing the Revolutionary War. At a restaurant, a woman of about eighty told me that Dr. Samuel Prescott, to whom she is related, deserves more credit than he has been given for completing Paul Revere's ride to Concord. The counterman at the hotel entered into the spirit of the occasion, too. After advising guests to be at Lexington Green by 4:30 in the morning to secure a good vantage point, he told a "well-known story around here" about Paul Revere stopping at every tavern for a drink on his way to Lexington.

It feels eerie, as I learned on the morning of the nineteenth, to leave a hotel at 4:15 A.M. to join hundreds of people walking like ghosts through the darkness. I found a good place by the roped-off green and stood beneath the stars with the waiting crowd. At about 5:10 the first traces of morning light revealed that people had climbed into trees and onto rooftops to watch the battle. A few minutes later I could see well enough to make out individual faces.

People of all ages were there—high school students, parents with young children, and elderly men and women. Many of them wore minuteman T-shirts and three-cornered hats, and a few had dressed in complete revolutionary-era costumes to witness the reenactment. As the moment for the battle approached, everyone seemed to be talking history. A boy behind me proudly told his parents what he had learned at school about "Paul Bunyan's ride." Elsewhere, parents and children could be heard talking about John Hancock, Samuel Adams, and Captain John Parker, while a couple of history buffs competed with each other at relating "little-known facts" about the battle.

Suddenly a young man portraying William Diamond came out

their power to RESIST THEM.

" Be firm my friends, nor let UNMANLY SLOTH
Twine round your hearts indiffoluble chains.
Ne'er yet by *force* was *freedom* overcome.
Unlefs CORRUPTION firft dejects the pride,
And guardian vigour of the free-born foul,
All crude attempts of *violence* are vain.
                                    Determined, hold
Your INDEPENDENCE; for, that *once deftroy'd,*
Unfounded Freedom is a morning dream."
    The liberties of our Country, the freedom of our
civil conftitution are worth defending at all hazards :
And it is our duty to defend them againft all attacks.
We have receiv'd them as a fair Inheritance from our
worthy Anceftors; They purchas'd them for us with
toil and danger and expence of treafure and blood ; and
tranfmitted them to us with care and diligence. It will
bring an everlafting mark of infamy on the prefent generation, enlightned as it is, if we fhould fuffer them
to be wrefted from us by violence without a ftruggle ;
or be cheated out of them by the artifices of falfe and
defigning men. Of the latter we are in moft danger at
prefent : Let us therefore be aware of it. Let us con-
template our forefathers and pofterity ; and refolve to
maintain the rights bequeath'd to us from the former,
for the fake of the latter.—Inftead of fitting down fa-
tisfied with the efforts we have already made, *which is*
the wifh of our enemies, the neceffity of the times, more
than ever, calls for our utmoft circumfpection, delibe-
ration, fortitude and perfeverance. Let us remember,
that " if we fuffer tamely a lawlefs attack upon our
liberty, we encourage it, and involve others in our doom".
It is a very ferious confideration, which fhould deeply
imprefs our minds, that *millions yet unborn may be the*
miferable fharers in the event.
                                    CANDIDUS.

Writing as Candidus in the Boston Gazette *of October 14, 1771,*
Samuel Adams refers to us as "millions yet unborn" in the second line
from the bottom.

onto the green and began beating his drum. The Lexington militiamen, looking exactly as I had pictured, rushed to the green to answer his call. There were teenage boys among them, and others the age of grandfathers. As Dolly Quincy said, they made a sorry sight standing there in the damp grass wearing their old farm clothes and shouldering an assortment of weapons. Yet there was something about our troops that stirred the soul, and I'm certain that many of us in the crowd of three thousand had to wipe away a tear just looking at them.

Around 5:30 a patriot on horseback rode up shouting that the redcoats were coming. A short time later they appeared, looking so menacing that a few children in the crowd screamed. "Disperse, ye rebels!" Major Pitcairn shouted. I couldn't blame those militiamen who did begin to disperse—they had no chance against the redcoats waiting with their weapons gleaming in the rising sun. But then a shot was fired—from where I couldn't tell. Suddenly a tremendous flurry of shots rang out, echoing and reechoing off the buildings as the smell of powder filled the air. A few of our troops fell. Others ran in confusion. But some stood their ground against the hopeless odds and returned the fire as the crowd cheered the first American resistance of the Revolution.

Walking back through Lexington on that spring morning, I thought of Samuel Adams watching the real battle with John Hancock from a distance and wondered what he would think of the reenactment. I think I know the answer. Samuel would be very proud to know that, more than two hundred years later, Americans still celebrate the start of our fight for independence. If he could see it, he might even say: "What a glorious morning is this!"

Acknowledgments and Picture Credits

Picture Research by Judith Bloom Fradin

For their help, the author thanks:

Philip Abbott, Technical Services Librarian, New Hampshire Historical Society; Philip Bergen, Librarian, the Bostonian Society; Robert S. Katz, M.D.; Lexington (Massachusetts) Historical Society; New England Historic and Genealogical Society; Sue Ohlson, Interlibrary Loan Librarian, Niles (Illinois) Public Library.

For the use of illustrations on the following pages the author thanks the:

American Antiquarian Society: pages 40, 82, 119, 173

Boston Beer Company Limited Partnership: page 168 (SAMUEL ADAMS BOSTON LAGER plus design is a registered trademark of the Boston Beer Company Limited Partnership.)

Boston Museum of Fine Arts: Jacket front

Library of Congress: pages ii, 2, 4, 5, 7, 9, 11, 19, 24, 27, 29, 31, 35, 38, 41, 48, 49,, 53, 56, 64, 65, 66, 67, 72, 76, 80, 86, 89, 93, 97, 99, 100, 103, 104, 105, 106, 109, 112, 114, 115, Jacket back and 122, 123, 124,125, 130, 131, 133, 138, 150, 154, 162

Massachusetts Historical Society: pages 22, 69, 156

National Archives: pages 15, 121, 132, 134

National Portrait Gallery, Smithsonian Institution: page 144

New York Public Library: pages 127, 159

Stock Montage, Chicago: pages x, 14, 32, 79

Bibliography

Alderman, Clifford Lindsey. *Samuel Adams: Son of Liberty*. New York: Holt, Rinehart and Winston, 1961.

Canfield, Cass. *Samuel Adams's Revolution*. New York: Harper & Row, 1976.

Chidsey, Donald Barr. *The World of Samuel Adams*. Nashville: Thomas Nelson, 1974.

Fischer, David Hackett. *Paul Revere's Ride*. New York: Oxford University Press, 1994.

Fleming, Thomas. *The First Stroke: Lexington, Concord, and the Beginning of the American Revolution*. Washington, D.C.: National Park Service, 1978.

Hall-Quest, Olga W. *Guardians of Liberty: Sam Adams and John Hancock*. New York: Dutton, 1963.

Hosmer, James K. *Samuel Adams*. Boston: Houghton Mifflin, 1899.

Lewis, Paul. *The Grand Incendiary: A Biography of Samuel Adams*. New York: Dial, 1973.

Miller, John C. *Sam Adams: Pioneer in Propaganda*. Stanford,California: Stanford University Press, 1960.

Wagner, Frederick. *Patriot's Choice: The Story of John Hancock*. New York: Dodd, Mead, 1964.

Wells, William V. *Life and Public Services of Samuel Adams* (3 volumes). Boston: Little, Brown, 1866 (reprinted 1969).

Index